For information address:

SAGE PUBLICATIONS, INC.
275 South Beverly Drive
Beverly Hills, California 90212

SAGE PUBLICATIONS LTD
St George's House / 44 Hatton Garden
London EC1N 8ER

International Standard Book Number 0-8039-0540-8

Library of Congress Catalog Card No. 75-9043

FIRST PRINTING

When citing a professional paper, please use the proper form. Remember to cite the
correct Sage Professional Paper series title and include the paper number. One of the
two following formats can be adapted (depending on the style manual used):

(1) NAGEL, S. S. (1973) "Comparing Elected and Appointed Judicial Systems."
Sage Professional Papers in American Politics, 1, 04-001. Beverly Hills, and London:
Sage Pubns.

OR

(2) Nagel, Stuart S. 1973. *Comparing Elected and Appointed Judicial Systems.* Sage
Professional Papers in American Politics, vol. 1, series no. 04-001. Beverly Hills and
London: Sage Publications.

Series / Number 04-028

Minimum Coalitions
in Legislatures:
A Review of the Evidence

DONALD S. LUTZ
University of Houston

JAMES R. WILLIAMS
Texas A&M University

SAGE PUBLICATIONS / Beverly Hills / London

CONTENTS

Minimum Coalitions in Legislatures: A Review of the Evidence

DONALD S. LUTZ
University of Houston

JAMES R. WILLIAMS
Texas A&M University

INTRODUCTION

Political coalition theory, like other scientific theories, seeks to provide explanations for political phenomena through formulation of an explicit logical calculus. The validity of such analysis is determined by empirically testing nonobvious operational hypotheses deduced from the logical system. Thus in evaluating coalition theory, criticism may be based either on examination of the formal statements for defects in logic, or on the results of empirical tests. Both are required for satisfactory scientific inquiry, however a purely theoretical critique such as that made by Robert Butterworth (1971) has different implications than an empirical test such as that made by Murray and Lutz (1974). In the first instance the critique may illustrate fundamental logical problems such that the theory, qua theory, is destroyed. In the second instance, negative results simply deny the utility of the theory on that set of political phenomena. While analysis may indicate the possible utility of another model using different assumptions, the original model is still logically intact and available for use elsewhere.

We will focus in this paper on the body of literature which emphasizes the second kind of evaluation. That is we will look primarily at empirical

AUTHORS' NOTE: *We would like to express our appreciation to Howard M. Leichter and Richard W. Murray for their helpful comments. A version of this essay was originally presented at the 1974 annual meeting of the American Political Science Association, Chicago, Illinois.*

tests of coalition theory. More specifically, we shall examine empirical tests of coalition theory which attempt to assay its utility in ordering legislative data. Because research on coalition formation in American legislagures has tended to emphasize Riker's work, our review of the literature will inevitably involve an evaluation of his model's utility, although other models will be evaluated as well.[1]

Our purpose in reviewing the empirical literature on coalition formation is to systematically compile the findings and assess the utility of any minimum coalition theory in light of these findings. We will be led to conclude that none of the prominent candidates, including Riker's model, are very useful in the legislative context. Instead, the empirical literature consistently points toward a model that treats minimum-sized winning coalitions as a special case.

Within the empirical literature on coalition formation there is a further distinction, namely the distinction between research on European multiparty systems and research on American national and state legislatures. The distinction is important not because research in one context is unrelated to research in the other, but rather because research in the parliamentary context can shed light on the direction for future research in the American context. Thus, although our ultimate concern in this effort is the status of coalition theory with respect to American legislatures, we shall begin with discussion of the literature on parliamentary systems.

THE PARLIAMENTARY CONTEXT

Eric C. Browne (1973) has already done an excellent job of summarizing this part of the literature, and much of our discussion for the next few pages will rely on his monograph. Browne divides all theories of coalition behavior into two categories. The first focuses on payoff maximization by rational actors. Basically it is hypothesized that the payoff distribution is a function of player "weight"—weight being the resources a player brings into the game, usually measured in terms of how many votes the player has. Thus, weight becomes the explanatory or independent variable and coalition size becomes the dependent variable. Browne identified Riker (1962), Gamson (1962; 1961a; 1961b), and Leiserson (1968; 1966) as major representatives of this group, although some of Leiserson's work falls in the next category.

The second set of theories derived from game theory and from a similar intellectual tradition can be distinguished by its insistence that a policy dimension be included as an explanatory variable in addition to player weight. Sometimes termed "policy distance" at other times "ideological distance," it amounts to the notion that coalition partners will be chosen not only on the basis of short-term payoff maximization—for example, the number of ministries held—but also long-term payoff maximization, that is, the ability to pass and enforce certain policies because your coalition partners are in basic agreement, or not hostile, to such policies. Browne identifies Axelrod (1972), DeSwaan (1970), Taylor (1972), and some of Leiserson's work (1970) as representative of this second category. One might also add Damgaard (1972), Flanagan (1973), and Browne himself (1973: 72), who concludes that:

> The value of belonging to a particular winning coalition is not related in any necessary way to its size alone. It is, rather, more accurately assessed as being a function of the amount of agreement existing between the preferences of players regarding the implementation of some set of proposals or ongoing programs.

As he points out, using only "weights" as the independent variable leads Riker, Gamson, and Leiserson to deduce that a rational actor would always produce a minimum-sized winning coalition. Regardless of which definition one uses for "minimum," Browne concludes that "minimum-sized winning coalitions do not form frequently in our universe"—the universe being the winning coalitions formed in 13 parliamentary systems between 1945 and 1969 (Browne, 1973: 54). While he does establish that regardless of a coalition's size the percentage share of ministries received will be proportional on a one-to-one basis with its percentage share of coalition seats, Browne presents no empirical evidence that policy distance is the explanatory variable missing—although he provides strong logical reasons as well as pointing to DeSwaan's work.

Abraham DeSwaan (1970) develops a theory of policy distance minimization with data drawn from politics in four European parliaments and compares its ability to explain coalition formation with that of Leiserson's theory. DeSwaan is more successful at predicting winning coalitions, but he does so primarily because he generates a larger set of predicted coalitions. This fact vitiates the utility of DeSwaan's theory and leaves Browne's conclusion seemingly without support. However, recent work has consistently pointed toward policy distance as a crucial variable.

Robert Axelrod (1972), for example, develops a "conflict of interest" model of coalitions formation that in effect is based on policy distance minimization. His key assumption is that conflict of interest is proportional to policy distance, so that in minimizing conflict one must minimize policy distance (1972: 169). Thus, he posits that winning coalitions will not only be minimal but "connected." So, for example, if we take the situation below of a parliament with 65 seats which requires a majority of 33 seats to form a government, and assume that six parties are rank ordered from left to right, CDF is a minimal winning coalition. However, it is not ideologically connected, whereas BC and CDE are both minimal

Party	Number of seats
A	6
B	15
C	26
D	5
E	11
F	2

and connected. A minimal connected winning coalition (MCW coalition) is:

(1) a coalition consisting of adjacent members (minimum policy distance),

(2) a winning coalition, and

(3) minimal in the sense that the loss of any one party results in its defeat.

The result is a set of predictions quite different than those generated by Riker's theory, since the MCW coalition is often considerably larger than what Riker would term minimum. For example, in the above situation Riker would predict coalition CDF or BDEF since they total 33 out of 65, whereas Axelrod would predict BC (41 seats) or CDE (42 seats).

Examining the 17 cabinets formed in Italy between 1953 and 1969, Axelrod found that 10 were minimal connected winning coalitions but only three were minimal in the Rikerian sense. It is worth noting that both Riker and Axelrod averaged only two or three predictions for each of the events, and two of the three predicted correctly by Riker were also predicted by Axelrod. Thus, Axelrod's theory is not vitiated in the way that DeSwaan's was by a large number of predictions; it is still clearly superior to Riker's theory in ordering this particular set of data.

Axelrod's work differs not only in degree from Riker's, it also differs in kind since it is not based on a strong assumption of rationality, and does not assume a zero-sum situation. On the contrary, Axelrod concludes that, "The comparison tends to reinforce the point that in studying a situation that is inherently non-zero-sum, the application of a zero-sum theory may not be very successful" (1972: 180). We will consider the implications of these proposals for studying coalitions in American legislatures in a later section.

Scott Flanagan (1973) similarly stresses policy distance, although he uses the term "dissonance costs" to indicate what Axelrod means by conflict of interest. Flanagan is more complex in his approach, however, in that he takes into account not only policy distance but also issue salience. In a sophisticated analysis of coalition crisis situations in eight countries his theory predicted 24 out of 30 cases (80%) and in about half of these (16 out of 30) he actually predicted the specific coalition that was formed. He concludes that the notion of a minimum winning coalition is of limited value. Rather, a coalition theory must include the dissonance principle (policy distance minimization) and a unanimity principle to explain the incidence of the entire range of coalition sizes. He operationalizes the unanimity principle as "ruling potential." In effect, he argues that a coalition must not only form a cabinet but have the inherent ability to actually rule effectively. Thus, considerations of policy distance and the need to placate the opposition combine to create pressures for larger than minimum-sized coalitions. This introduces the concept of bargaining and, as he notes, means assuming a non-zero-sum situation (Flanagan, 1973: 297). Finally, he implies that the *content* and salience of the issue for the parties will have an important effect on coalition formation.

One more effort in the parliamentary context needs to be examined before moving to the American legislative context. Erik Damgaard found that in the Danish Folketing between 1953 and 1970 "minimal majority behavior (was) not adopted by the parties as a principle strategy in law making," but in those instances where a roll-call was not unanimous virtually 90% of the coalitions are "explained" by a unidimensional model. That is to say, Damgaard found that rank-ordering the major parties according to a traditional left-wing ideological dimension resulted in "connected" winning coalitions being formed 90% of the time—"connected" here having the same meaning as that advanced by Axelrod. Clearly we have one more instance where policy distance is shown to be an important variable. Furthermore, Damgaard tested the impact of issue content and found that the propensity for minimal-sized winning coalitions is strongly affected by issue content. That minimal-sized winning coalitions were typically found on tax bill divisions further undercuts the probable utility of a zero-sum assumption since "most tax bills involve tax increases, and it is hard to imagine that a tax increase in any sensible way can represent 'payoff' to governing parties (Damgaard, 1972: 38).

To summarize, the literature on coalition formation in the parliamentary context suggests the following conclusions:

(1) *Any useful theory of coalition formation* will need to account for the entire range of coalition sizes, not just those of a minimal size, since minimal-size coalitions, regardless of the definition of "minimal" being used, occur relatively infrequently.

(2) *Minimal-size theories of coalition formation,* including Riker's, are not very useful in the parliamentary context and should be replaced by spatial models not assuming a zero-sum situation.

(3) *Aside from eschewing a zero-sum assumption,* models which appear useful in a parliamentary context do not need to assume perfect information or make a strong assumption of rationality.

(4) *Policy distance* appears to be a crucial independent variable in the parliamentary context in addition to player "weight," and therefore any useful theory of coalition formation must be multivariate.

(5) *Issue content,* because it determines whether or not the policy distance variable is activated, appears also to be an important variable for explaining coalition size as well as who belongs to the coalition.

The evidence is not conclusive, but is is strong, it is consistent, and it is all we have at this time.[2]

THE AMERICAN LEGISLATIVE CONTEXT

When we look at research in the American context there is also considerable consistency in the findings, but there is some division among researchers as to how these findings should be interpreted. We will first outline the findings and then take a closer look at the nature and source of that disagreement.

Unlike the parliamentary context, where Riker's model is one of several prominent theories tested, the American legislative context finds empirical research on coalition formation focusing heavily on Riker's proposal. For this reason an examination of research on American legislatures necessarily becomes at the same time an evaluation of the applicability of Riker's theory.

David W. Moore's article (1969) tests Riker's proposition that coalitions larger than majority will shed members to minimize payoff costs and thus always tend toward minimalness. Using roll-call data from the Indiana House of Representatives between 1923 and 1963, Moore assumes that the majority party during that time period always served as the proto-coalition in the bargaining process. He hypothesizes that if Riker were correct, the tendency for larger than minimal winning coalitions to drop unneeded members would be reflected in a declining average voting cohesion as the size of the majority party increases. That is, if Riker were correct, there should be a negative relationship between majority party size and that party's voting cohesion. In fact, Moore found no systematic relationship between size and cohesion. Introduction of a series of control variables did not change the initial result in any significant fashion.

Seeking to find a set of roll-calls that best fit Riker's conditions, Moore then refined his sample to include only those roll-calls on which a majority of one party cast votes opposed to a majority of the other party. Since these matters are hotly contested along party lines it is assumed that they related to control of the House and thus are close to meeting the zero-sum condition. Looking only at this refined sample Moore finds the negative relationship between size and cohesion, but concludes that Riker's model is still not supported since the net effect of increasing size on the probability that the coalition will be successful is still positive. That is, where Riker (1962: 66) predicts declining cohesion associated with increasing coalition size will lead to internal conflicts decreasing the effectiveness of the winning coalition, Moore finds that as the coalition gets larger in a zero-sum situation it does indeed become less cohesive but the effectiveness of the coalition still continues to increase.

The decisiveness of this negative result is clouded somewhat by the indirect connection between the operationalized variables and Riker's predictions. For example, it is not clear that what Moore calls "effectiveness" would be accepted by Riker. Moore himself admits that "bills that were passed by a small majority may have been substantively more important than those passed by large majorities" (1969: 1078). Thus, larger majorities may be passing more bills but these bills could be so watered down that they present little or no payoff to anyone. Also, William Bicker (1968: 67-75) reaches contrary conclusions using the same data base, although there is no systematic refutation of Moore, and until a specific cuunter-test using the same data appears in print Moore's work must be accepted. Whether or not Moore has disproven Riker's hypothesis linking size and effectiveness, his work clearly implies that issue content is a variable to be studied. Some issues induce a more zero-sum response than others, and sometimes the proto-coalition retains its cohesion while at other times it does not. There is also the implicit assumption that party membership is a variable to be considered which may introduce considerations of ideology.

Barbara Hinckley (1972) conducts a similar test of the relationship between party size and coalition cohesion using roll-call data from the 81st through 91st Congresses. However, she explictly introduces the notion of "ideological distance." She argues that there are natural forces operating in a legislature to make coalitions larger than minimal. Among these are:

(1) seriality—coalitions are not independent but are part of a continuing process in which accommodation for future gains must be taken into account;

(2) open entry—coalition leaders cannot prevent individuals from joining for their own reasons and thus inflating the size of the coalition; and

(3) strong consensual norms.

Drawing explicitly from the work of Leiserson and DeSwaan she hypothesizes that in a legislature structured along party lines there are policy costs in seeking votes across party lines. Thus coalition leaders have an incentive not only to maximize party support of the coalition but also to limit membership to party members in order to minimize ideological distance. She concludes that as party size increases so will coalition sizes but, contrary to Riker, she predicts cohesion will not decline.

Her data support the conclusion that there is no tendency for minimum-sized winning coalitions to form. Coalitions do increase in size well above minimum with increasing party strength, although at a decreasing rate. She also argues that ideological distance is an important variable for explaining the decreasing rate in the increasing size of coalitions.

Hinckley's findings must be considered tentative for two reasons. First, other research, as she points out, does not match hers although none gives support for Riker's hypotheis. Moore, as shown earlier, finds a negative relationship between size and cohesion under certain circumstances. Wayne Francis (1970) found some negative correlation in the Indiana legislature, although sessions with large majorities were associated with high cohesion. Hugh LeBlanc (1969) found no relation between cohesion and size in the 26 different state senates he examined. These do not vitiate Hinckley's findings but caution against excessive interpretation until the conditions producing the differential results are better understood, as Hinckley herself admits (1972: 207). Second, and more important, Hinckley's decision to limit her data set to roll-calls where majorities in each party opposed each other biases her set of votes toward matters where party voting prevails. That is, her data set is based on roll-calls where cohesion is by definition high and thus exposes her to the charge that her logic is circular. Again, her conclusions are not invalidated but they cannot be considered decisive.

Eric Uslaner (1974) makes another attempt to test this aspect of Riker's theory. Using House roll-call data from the 80th to the 91st Congresses, he tests the hypothesis that party defection will increase as the size of the majority party increases, although he derives the proposal from Sorauf's work showing it to be logically related to Riker's predictions.

His findings are negative. However, he goes one step further and suggests that the perfect information assumption can be relaxed. Both Sarah McCally (1966) and Adrian and Press (1968) have suggested using 55% rather 50%+1 to define a minimal winning coalition. Their reasoning is precisely the same as that used by Axelrod and Riker, namely that in the face of uncertainty coalition builders are likely to "pad" their proto-coalitions to be relatively certain of victory. Axelrod terms this the "modi-fied version of Riker's theory" and it is one of the alternatives he tests and rejects in his study. Using a second-order polynomial regression on what he terms the "McCally thesis," Uslaner also rejects this version of the size principle. His conclusion differs from Hinckley's, however, in that he finds in both instances no relationship between party size and the degree of cohesion in the House.

In another study based upon his data, Uslaner (1973) reports that one variable usually neglected by researchers does bring some order to the variance, and that is the subject matter of the roll-calls. He finds that on "bread and butter" issues of a nonideological nature, such as budgetary matters, the pattern of partisan coalition formation appears to be cyclical with both parties being most cohesive in the Congresses immediately pre-ceeding presidential elections involving incumbents. The pattern is dif-ferent on questions with a higher ideological content such as civil rights and antipoverty legislation. Thus, while rejecting Hinckley's finding of the relationship between coalition size and cohesion, he musters empirical support for her contention that ideology is an important consideration in studying coalition formation. There appears then to be a growing consen-sus that Riker's theory is not useful in the American legislative context, doubt that any theory using a zero-sum assumption will be useful, and indications that policy distance (ideology) and issue content are important variables for explaining coalition behavior. While the evidence at this point is cumulative it is not yet conclusive.

Two recent articles by Richard Murray and Donald Lutz attempt to test Riker's model directly by uncovering legislative situations where Riker's conditions are most closely approximated. Having concluded with others that the zero-sum assumption is not realistic in a legislature where coalitions are serial rather than independent, and that perfect information is not a reasonable assumption given politics in American legislatures, Murray and Lutz seek to find some subset of legislative decisions which will be characterized by zero-sumness and a high level of information in order to conduct a "strong" test of the minimum-size coalition hypothesis. In the first article (Murray and Lutz, 1974) they focus on redistricting decisions in the states since 1900. An obvious (extreme) situation where legislators maximize their information occurs when their legislative house

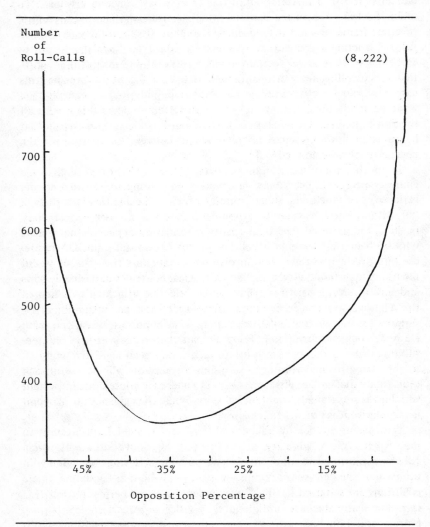

Figure 1: TEXAS ROLL-CALL TOTALS: ALL SESSIONS[a]

[a] Reproduced from Lutz and Murray, as are figures 2, 3, and 4.

is being redistricted and their own seats are in jeopardy. Furthermore, the situation is by definition zero-sum since, even when a couple of seats are added, it is still a matter of someone loses what someone else gets. To make the test stronger the sample of available redistricting roll-calls within the time-frame selected is reduced to the closest roll-call for each successful redistricting plan, but even with this subset intentionally biased to favor Riker there is no general tendency toward minimum winning coalitions. Controlling for the qualitative nature of the redsitricting plan, the extent of redistricting, and the size of the voting body only marginally improve the results. However, Murray and Lutz find a distinct positive relationship between the degree of interparty competition within the legislature and the proportion of winning redistricting coalitions which approach the minimum size.

In the second article (Lutz and Murray, 197X) the same authors examine more than 12,000 roll-calls covering the full range of recorded votes in the Texas House and Senate during the 1960s. Their first observation, one that will be confirmed by David Koehler (1972b) in other legislatures, is that minimal-sized coalitions as described by Riker occur rather infrequently across the range of issues. The distribution of roll-calls is U-shaped, or bi-modal, with more than two-thirds having less than 5% of voting members in the opposition, as shown in Figure 1. Lutz and Murray then focus their attention on the subset of roll-calls having at least 15% opposition. Within this truncated sample they find that there is variance in the distribution of winning coalition sizes from session to session, suggesting historical or structural changes in the legislature as possible variables (see Figure 2).

Two structural features are focused upon in an attempt to uncover the source of variance. Some sessions were followed by special sessions during which important and highly controversial bills were faced in a setting largely devoid of the myriad of small, routine measures. It is to be expected that under such circumstances the level of information would be much higher and legislators would be more involved in the outcome. Each special sessions was sorted out from its respective session to see if this accounted for variance in the tendency toward minimal-sized winning coalitions between sessions. Surprisingly the roll-call distribution for the special sessions was in each case indistinguishable from that of the respective regular session as exemplified in Figure 3. If the assumption of higher information level is a fair one, then this constitutes further evidence against Riker's prediction.

A second feature of the Texas legislature is the requirement for a four-fifths majority on certain kinds of roll-calls. Approximately every seventh roll-call is of this variety and it is to be expected that since an extraordi-

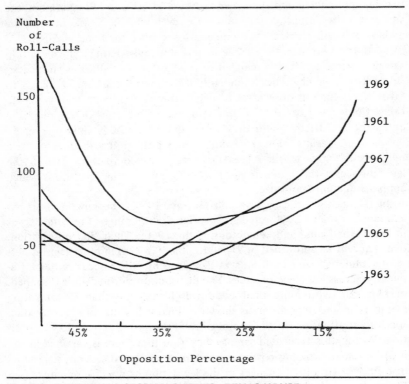

Figure 2: **INDIVIDUAL SESSION CURVES: TEXAS HOUSE**

nary majority is difficult to achieve there will be a stronger tendency toward minimalness since the payoffs are being severely eroded. In fact,
Lutz and Murray find that the distribution on such roll-calls is less inclined toward minimalness than on ordinary roll-calls as is illustrated in
Figure 4.

Some speculation as to the source of between-session variance is in-
dulged in, but the balance of the article deals with an examination of the
impact of issue content on coalition size. An attempt is made to identify
those policy areas that would most closely approximate Riker's implied
condition of divisibility of a universally valued payoff contingent upon
victory. Only where such payoffs are available to coalition leaders to dis-
tribute among members of the winning side does Riker's formulation predict the creation of minimum winning coalitions. The expected relationship between the divisibility of payoffs and winning coalition size is not
found. In fact, the greatest tendency toward minimum winning coalitions

appears on those roll-calls characterized by the presumed absence of divisible payoffs. Specifically, those roll-calls with a high ideological content such as civil rights bills, resolutions dealing with the war in Vietnam, and so forth, are almost twice as likely to produce a minimum coalition as those in the next highest category. This matches Uslaner's findings for Congress and underlines further the probable importance of ideological distance as first noted by Hinckley.

David Koehler's research into coalition patterns in four state legislatures and the United States Congress produces findings congruent with those of Lutz and Murray. The distribution curves for Alabama, New Jersey, Tennessee, Wisconsin, and the United States House and Senate are generally U-shaped with relatively few roll-calls producing near-minimal coalitions, although in most instances the second highest mode is located at the minimal point. The opposition distribution curves from Koehler's findings are reproduced here to illustrate that Texas is not idiosyncratic,

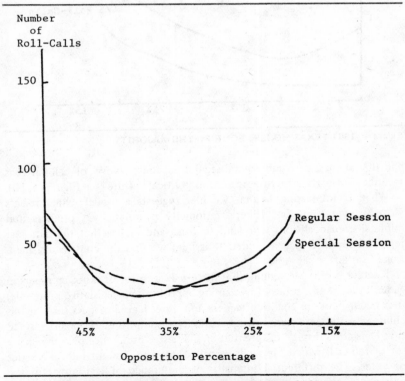

Figure 3: 1961 TEXAS HOUSE: REGULAR AND SPECIAL SESSION

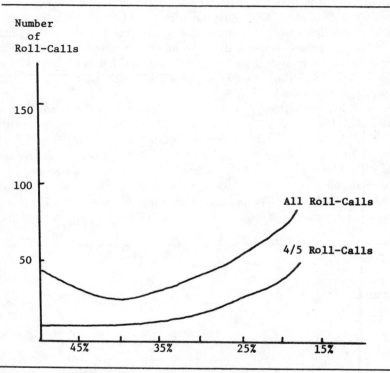

Figure 4: 1967 TEXAS HOUSE: FOUR-FIFTHS MAJORITY

and that there are certain general regularities in legislative roll-call patterns regardless of party structure, region, or political culture (see Figures 5-10).

What is interesting is that Koehler suggests a model which rejects virtually everything but Riker's rationality postulate, yet predicts that minimal-sized coalitions *will* tend to form and argues that the data just reported support such a model. It is here we find the controversy mentioned earlier.

Koehler begins by arguing that the legislative process is not an n-person game, but rather a series of bargaining opportunities (legislative proposals) that occur between coalition leaders and other legislators. As such he has eliminated the zero-sum and non-seriality assumptions. He posits instead that legislators display differential intensities of preference over the entire set of roll-calls which they will be called upon to demonstrate in a series of votes. The differential intensity of preference of legislators for the passage or defeat of any in the sequence of motions means that on any

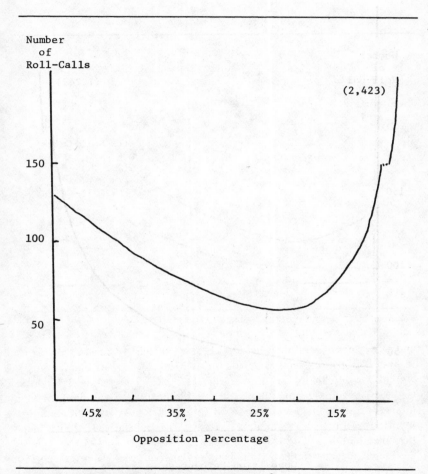

Figure 5: ALABAMA OPPOSITION DISTRIBUTION[a]

[a]Figures 5, 6, 7, 8, 9, 10, and 12 are reproduced from Koehler, 1972b.

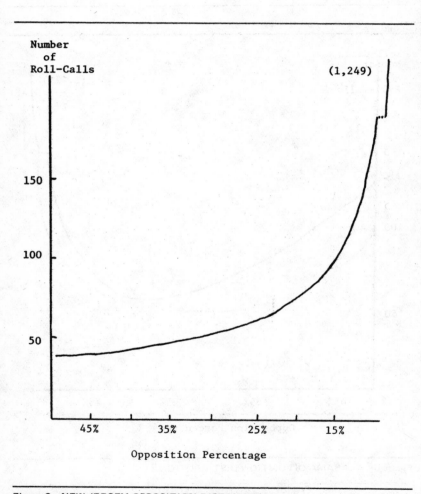

Figure 6: NEW JERSEY OPPOSITION DISTRIBUTION

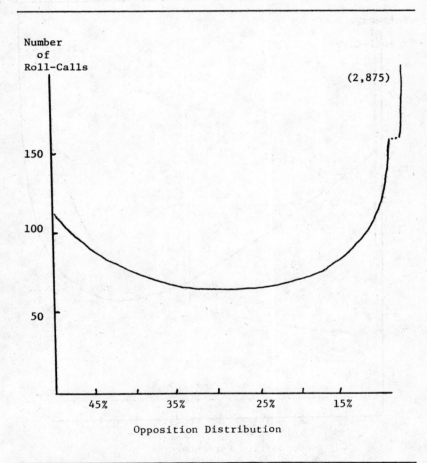

Figure 7: TENNESSEE OPPOSITION DISTRIBUTION

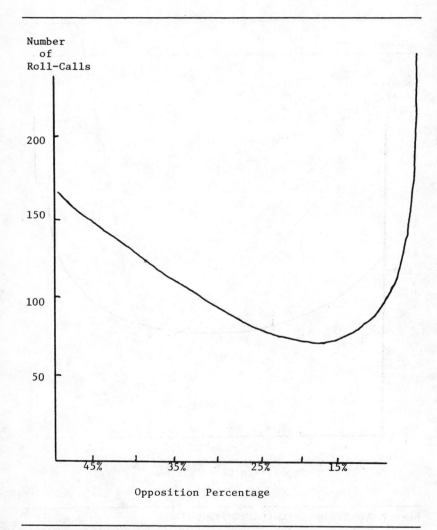

Figure 8: WISCONSIN OPPOSITION DISTRIBUTION

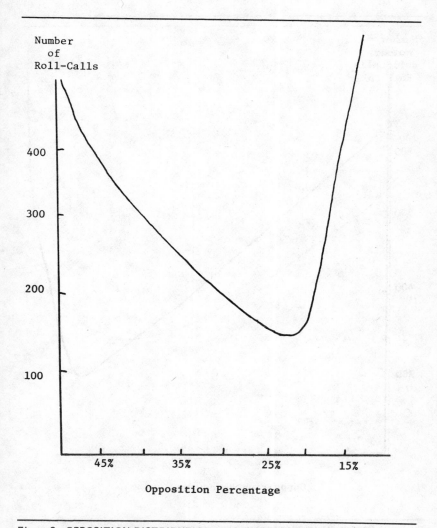

Figure 9: OPPOSITION DISTRIBUTION: U.S. HOUSE 1943-1968

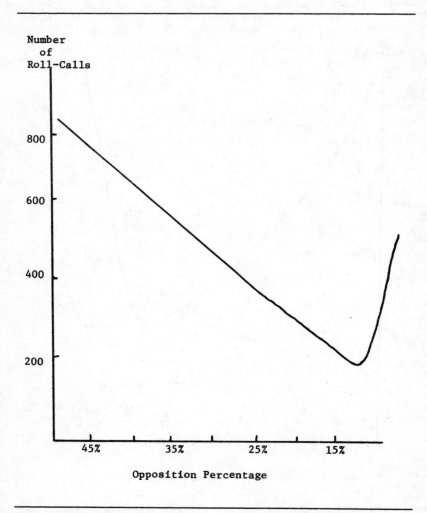

Figure 10: OPPOSITION DISTRIBUTION: U.S. SENATE 1937-1968

single motion it may be rational for some members to buy votes to assure victory on the roll-call while for others it will be rational to sell their votes. Of course, preferences and intensities on other roll-calls could reverse the relationship, and it is the bargaining among legislators in the attempt to achieve their respective preferences, especially those strongly held, that leads to rational behavior. Since the resources by which votes are bought and sold are scarce and must be economized for future roll-calls, any coalition builder will cease adding members as soon as he has assured himself of victory.

At this point Koehler rejects another Riker assumption—that of perfect information. Arguing, as many others have, that information possessed by legislators is imperfect, he concludes that coalition builders will tend strongly to seek that size which will *assure* victory, but no larger. One piece of information usually lacking is precisely how many legislators will in fact vote, but if a coalition builder creates a coalition which is a majority of the entire house then victory is assured. Thus, Koehler argues that the minimum-sized winning coalition is not a simple majority of those voting but a simple majority of the entire house. What is interesting is the consistency with which the data support such a model, at least upon an initial analysis. Table 1 summarizes the findings by Koehler and Lutz and Murray in the various arenas. Looking only at those roll-calls on which there were at least 15% in opposition, the percentage of the house voting, on the average, varies between 74.6% and 91.0% depending on the body. The average winning coalition varies in the same bodies between 63.9% and 68.8%—hardly a tendency toward minimal-sized coalitions. But if we compute the percentage these average coalitions comprise of the entire

TABLE 1
Summary Voting Pattern[a]

Voting Body	Percent Participation	Winners: Percent of Voters	Winners: Percent of Membership
U.S. House	84.2	63.9	53.8
U.S. Senate	82.2	65.4	53.7
Alabama	75.7	64.9	49.1
Tennessee	74.6	66.1	49.3
New Jersey	76.2	68.8	51.8
Wisconsin	88.4	65.2	57.7
Texas	91.0	64.3	57.9

[a]Roll-calls with at least 15% opposition.
Reproduced from Lutz and Murray.

body we find they tend to fall around a simple majority of the entire house, suggesting a strong preference for the coalition size Koehler predicts.

There are three problems with this conclusion. First of all, it is only one of several that can be supported by the data. A theory like Axelrod's or Flanagan's predicts larger than minimal-sized winning coalitions and also could claim comfort from the findings, So could, as we shall see, Martin Levein's model. The problem is that Koehler assumes what needs to be first established in an empirical, causal analysis—the intentions of coalition builders.

The second problem, one shared by Riker, is that in focusing on an explanation for the incidence of minimum-sized coalitions, Koehler apparently cannot explain the entire range of coalition sizes. Presumably, if a coalition builder has perfect information he will build the coalition Riker predicts—a bare majority of those voting. As the level of information declines he will be tempted to build larger and larger coalitions to ensure victory until he is building coalitions equal to one-half plus one of the entire house. However, there is no motivation suggested for a coalition builder to construct a coalition larger than this—despite the fact that over two-thirds of all coalitions in the legislatures studied were larger.

Third, the conclusion is based on a comparison of mean coalition sizes, and the mean in this case is a misleading statistic. Take the case of the Texas legislature for example. The mean roll-call had 64% of those voting in the winning coalition, or about 58% of the total house membership. If coalition leaders had consistently aimed at 58% of the total membership there should be a central tendency in coalition sizes centered around this point. Figure 11 superimposes this predicted curve on an actual curve.

The 58% line falls in the middle of the trough between the two modes in the bi-modal distribution. This fact, however, is not decisive in disproving Koehler's claim since there is enough variance in the number of legislators voting for the counterargument to suffer from the same problems—the simple statistic for central tendency may hide more than it reveals.

A more useful approach is to plot the number of roll-calls in terms of actual number in the winning coalition, since this more directly tests the extent to which coalitions tend in size toward one-half the membership of the entire house. Koehler found that in the case of the Tennessee legislature (see Figure 12) and the United States Congress, the curve does in fact have a pronounced mode near this point.

However, despite similar mean winning coalition size (see Table 1), a contrary pattern emerges for the two houses of the Texas legislature. In the case of the Senate only one session has a peak near 16, which is the

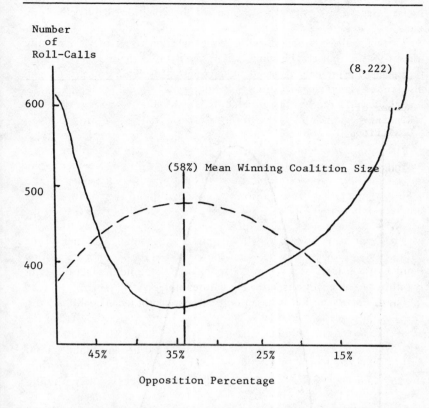

Figure 11: TEXAS HOUSE ROLL-CALL TOTALS: ALL SESSIONS WITH CURVE PREDICTED BY KOEHLER[a]

[a]Based on number of those actually voting. The average winning coalition has 64% of those voting and thus 36% opposition as shown above, which equals 58% of the entire House.

simple majority in the 31-member body (see Figure 13), and this is not the mode. In each case the mode is around 21 or 22—that is, half way between a majority of the Senate and the cutoff point for 15% opposition. There is no support for Koehler's prediction in the Texas Senate data.

The results in the House are more ambiguous (see Figure 14). All but one session are described by essentially flat curves with their mode somewhere between 90 and 100—well above the simple majority point for the 150-member body. The 1961 session, on the other hand, matches Koehler's prediction, and since the 1961 House had by far the largest

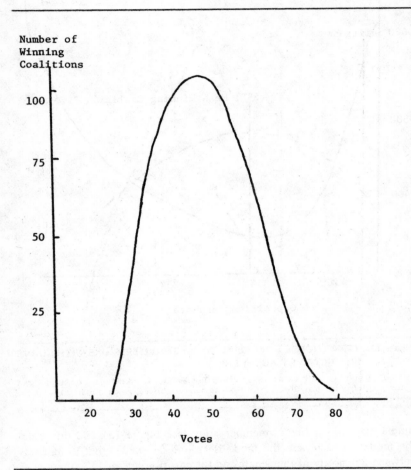

Figure 12: TENNESSEE WINNING COALITION DISTRIBUTION[a]

[a]Includes all roll-calls with 15% opposition in a body with 100 members.

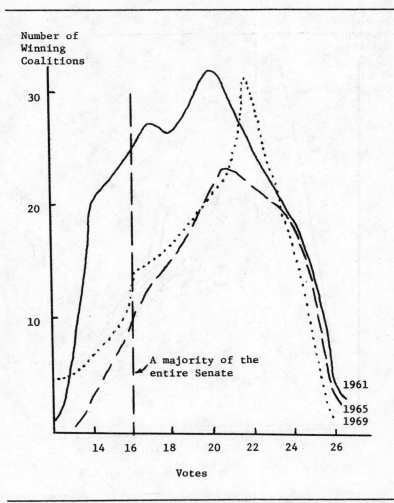

Figure 13: TEXAS SENATE WINNING COALITION DISTRIBUTION[a]

[a]Includes all roll-calls with 15% of more opposition.

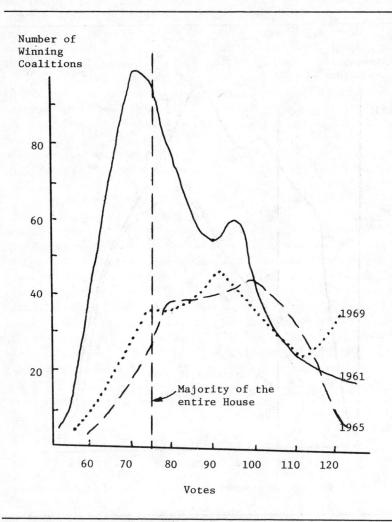

Figure 14: TEXAS HOUSE WINNING COALITION DISTRIBUTION[a]

[a]Includes all roll-calls with 15% of more opposition.

number of closely divided votes this would appear to bear Koehler out.[3] A careful analysis, however, leads to another conclusion.

Closely divided votes (those that differ by about 10 or less between winner and loser) are found almost exclusively in roll-calls where the winning coalition was between 50 and 80 members large, and 80% of these closely divided votes had less than 75 on the winning side. If coalition leaders were trying to achieve a majority of the entire Texas House on close roll-calls during the 1960s they consistently missed.

Furthermore, if we focus on the 75 to 80 range we find that 35% of the roll-calls with winning coalitions of this size were closely divided compared to 25% of all contested roll-calls, but roll-calls with winning coalitions in the 60 to 70 range were closely divided 75% of the time. Indeed it is in this latter category that we find a majority of closely divided, controversial, hard-fought roll-calls, and it is here where we are most likely to find leaders trying to maximize payoff in the Rikerian sense. Unfortunately it is well below the majority of the entire House.

What does this all mean? For one thing it means that the large number of minimum-sized winning coalitions in the 1961 House (minimum-sized here defined as a majority of those voting and thus representing closely divided roll-calls) does not explain that dramatic peak in the winning coalition distribution. Rather, it explains why the area under the curve is extended further to the left of the 75 vote line. It also means that lumping sessions together in one curve as Koehler has done may be misleading. In the case of the Texas legislature such combination would have produced an overall curve much more favorable to Koehler's prediction in the case of the House, but that would result largely from the 1961 session having an extraordinary number of roll-calls so that between-session variance would be buried. The existence of this between-session variance plus the pattern of closely divided votes just reported means finally that we must look elsewhere to explain the prominent mode in the 1961 session.[4]

A likely explanation is to be found in a characterization of that session of the Texas House made by Lutz and Murray (forthcoming):

> The 1961 House was closely divided between "liberals" and "conservatives" and a Speaker elected with liberal votes presided. By contrast, in the 1969 session, a conservative Speaker and a small clique of supporters ran the House, brooking no opposition from the small liberal minority.

Only in the 1961 House did this coalition of liberals and moderates gain control, and in order to do this they needed a majority of the entire House to elect the Speaker and control the rules. Having worked together at the beginning of the session they naturally could be expected to vote together on other matters out of ideological affinity if not because the Speaker with his powerful tools held them together. No other session in the 1960s had such an alignment, and no other session had a remotely similar voting pattern. Hence, the 1961 House voting anomaly may best be explained by prior factional alignments based on ideological distance. Such a conclusion is obviously congruent with our general discussion thus far.

Still to be explained is why the Texas House and Senate should give so little support to Koehler's proposal while winning coalition distributions for the Tennessee legislature and United States Congress do. All we can do at this point is speculate, but if our assessment concerning the importance of policy distance and prior factional alignment is correct, then the tendency for a legislature to produce a winning coalition distribution with a mode at or near one-half of the entire House is evidence of strong factional alignment in that body. Usually this alignment will be in the form of political parties, in which case the central tendency predicted by Koehler will become more pronounced as the parties become more evenly divided and/or more highly disciplined. Where parties are not the basis of prior alignments—either because one party is overwhelmingly dominant or because there is no party discipline—then we will have to look for other bases of alignment.

There is some support for such a connection between party division and the incidence of minimum winning coalitions, other than that discussed above. In an article cited earlier (Murray and Lutz, 1974: 247-249), it was found that in a selected sample of roll-calls in 38 states those states with closely divided legislatures were twice as likely to approach minimalness in roll-calls as were those where one party had a sizable majority. Party division, in fact, explained twice as much variance as any other factor examined.

While this matter is speculative, the general conclusions to be drawn from this section are not. Empirical research in the American legislative context supports the conclusions reached at the end of our discussion of research in the parliamentary context. Again, the evidence is not conclusive, but except in certain side issues arising from Hinckley's work and Koehler's interpretation, the evidence is rather consistent. At least it is consistent and strong enough for us to be able to make reasonable suggestions for future research—a subject to which we now turn.

DIRECTIONS FOR FUTURE RESEARCH

It is interesting to note that as work on coalition formation has proceeded Riker's assumptions have gradually been turned into independent variables by researchers—except in the case of rationality. The problem with *assuming* rationality is that it can imply different goals at different times, a fact which Riker himself recognizes (1962: 17-18). Riker argues that there are some situations with several measurably different outcomes (payoffs), and rational behavior consists in choosing the larger payoff. The problem lies partly in assuming that what we mean by "larger payoff" is the same as that meant by legislators. Much of empirical research has been directed at finding those situations where rational behavior will be in evidence, but such an approach does not directly face the alternative goals and payoff structures summarized by the term "rationality." Riker's use of the concept is intuitively appealing, and while most political scientists studying American legislatures have concluded that this context is not one where Riker's model can be of assistance this does not necessarily mean rejection of the rationality postualte. The concept must first be more clearly operationalized and then made to face the data. Koehler has operationalized "larger payoff" in Rikerian terms and concludes that minimum winning coalitions are indeed sought, although of a different type than predicted by Riker. Unfortunately Koehler must assume the very point to be proven, as must the others studying coalition formation. In sum, while there is evidence that at some times in some legislatures coalition leaders will seek a majority of the entire house as their winning coalition, there is evidence that coalition leaders often do not seek such coalition sizes. But the important point is that even if there were an indisputable pattern one way or the other, the controversy between Koehler and Lutz and Murray will probably not be settled short of interviewing coalition leaders to determine what their goals are and whether the preference patterns imputed to them are in fact theirs.

The process will be more complicated than asking coalition leaders what they are trying to achieve—a majority of those voting, a majority of the House, or something else—although this will help a great deal. The entire matter matter of what constitutes "rational" behavior must be more thoroughly investigated, and what this might show is suggested by Lutz and Murray.

Although not a formal theory as much as it is a proposal that we alter our treatment of the assumption of rationality, the authors propose a view which results from the Texas legislative setting but may hold in a more general way to a broader range of coalition building arenas. It is asserted that the legislative process in Texas during the period examined was characterized by limited constituent concern but extreme concern on the part of legislators that the party leaders respond to their interests. In the absence of constituent pressure, party/lobby pressure on legislators was left uncontested thus creating the lopsided voting majorities observed in this effectively one-party legislature as most legislators "go along to get along." Minimal winning coalitions, then, result when an issue of relatively high ideological content comes along which generates a response or pressure from the heterogeneous constituencies. Thus, when minimum winning coalitions do appear they are more a function of pressure from divided constituencies than of "rationally" constructed voting coalitions.[5] In sum, "rational" behavior in the Texas legislature is sometimes defined as the legislator going along with the party leader (and thus the house leadership) in order to prevent his being excluded entirely from payoffs distributed by the leadership. At other times, when the constituency is alerted and active, "rational" behavior for a Texas legislator is not dependent on being in the winning coalition but rather depends on taking particular stands for home consumption. In neither case is the "payoff," strictly speaking, divisible, nor does the payoff attach to the specific coalition at hand. That is, payoffs are noncontingent and the rationality of the coalition building process is "indeterminate" with respect to gaols.[6]

Thus far in coalition research it has always been assumed by model builders that actors will choose more rather than less, will be efficient in matching means to ends, and will be consistent in doing so. What Lutz and Murray are proposing is not that legislators are irrational, but rather that what is rational behavior will shift within the same decision-making body according to the circumstances. Sometimes it is rational in the long run to be on the losing side, and thus far the assumption of rationality in the literature has "buried" this possibility. Rather than *assume* what constitutes rational behavior for a legislator it is perhaps necessary to empirically determine the impact of issue content with respect to his ideological preferences as well as those of his salient constituency. In the multi-party parliamentary context this automatically has been taken into account. Running as a candidate for a disciplined party means an MP's policy preferences and those of his salient constituency are more or less matched as a result of the party candidate selection process, and the party leadership can usually expect the membership to act with a high degree of determinateness. If some members do not behave in the expected manner there are effective sanctions available to party leaders. In the American legislative context what constitutes rational behavior for a legislator is usually not so obvious or straightforward. Therefore we must ask what the goals and preferences of legislative actors and leaders are, how their respective preference patterns relate (ideological distance) on the various matters before them (issue content), and then ask what constitutes rational behavior in this situation. Rational behavior in a one-party context probably does not match that in a two-party system, or in a multi-party system with strong party discipline.[7]

The research strategy this suggests is obvious and straightforward although difficult to execute. Instead of stressing post hoc analysis of variance in the dependent variable—behavior on roll-calls or in cabinet formation—we need first to measure the independent variables and that requires interviewing legislators. Such an approach has been avoided by political scientists who use game-theoretic tools for the peculiar reason that it is "atheoretical." For example, Browne argues (1973: 44) that "the interview strategy does not satisfy the requirements of theory in as much as it will not allow us to fix the decision point in a manner which is generalizable across situations, and hence, the theory is denied the ability to predict outcomes." This will come as a shock to those doing survey research or socialization studies in a cross-national context. Fortunately the statement is true only if there are no behavioral regularities to be found in which case modern political scientists, including those using game-theoretic approaches, will simply have to pack up and go home. It is precisely when we do have interview data that we will be able to predict the entire range of coalition behavior. Strangely enough, Browne concedes the very point at the end of his monograph (1973: 80) (1973: 80) when he says:

> What is necessary is that some set of actors indicate a rankng among some set of stimuli. In our context this means that political parties will need to evaluate all other political parties according to their perceptions of the overall policy similarity of these parties to their own policy positions. In view of the fact that individuals and not parties are perceiving agents, it will be necessary to obtain similarity rankings from a suitable sample of party MPs, and aggregate them to party perceptions of the other parties.

Since such data can be obtained only by interviewing legislators, Browne ends up reaching the same conclusion we do despite his earlier disclaimer.

The Lutz-Murray proposal can be stated in terms of the useful distinction between procedural rationality and substantive rationality (Riker and Ordeshook, 1973: 12-16). In the first case a social scientist assumes logical behavior is universal (a procedural assumption) and then attempts to determine what goals must have existed in order to lead logically to the behavior that resulted. In the second case the researcher assumes an actor has a given goal and thus will behave in a certain fashion. That is, in the second approach the researcher assumes both the goal and logical behavior, whereas in the first he assumes logical behavior but determines the goals

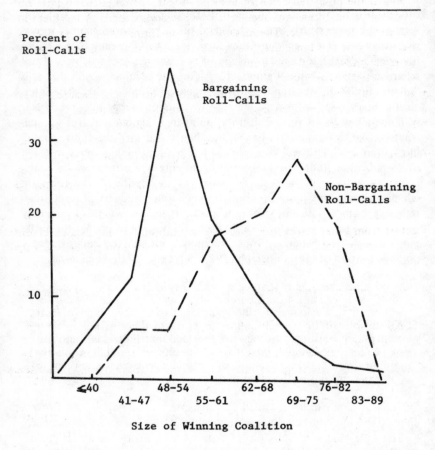

Figure 15: DISTRIBUTION OF WINNING COALITION SIZES FOR BARGAINING AND NON-BARGAINING ROLL-CALLS[a]

[a] Reproduced from Levine, 1971.

of an actor through his actual choices. Either approach will in the long run lead to an understanding of goals, although the method of substantive rationality also attempts to discover whether or not goals and behavior are logically related. A shortcoming with assuming substantive rationality is that if the predicted behavior does not occur, the researcher is not sure whether he has been incorrect in his attribution of goals or incorrect in his attribution of logic. Theories of coalition formation such as Riker's are usually of this type, and thus the negative empirical findings lead some to reject the assumption of rationality.[8] We do not reach such a conclusion. Rather we argue that the assumed goals in some coalition theories are incomplete in that one goal is assumed when there are several; when more than one is assumed not all major possibilities are included. Therefore we are recommending a shift to procedural rationality for the immediate future until further research clearly reveals what goals should be attributed and under what conditions. Only at that point will it be fruitful to assume substantive rationality.[9]

The task may not be as onerous as it once seemed. For example, David A. Karns (1974) has developed a program which, using an individual differences scaling approach, can indicate ideological distance of individual actors from other actors in a legislative setting thus serving as a check on our interview data. Indeed, the program can be used on roll-call data to map an entire legislature requiring only a random sample of interviews to confirm the pattern.

An important task at this point is to develop a theory which will meet the requirements set by the conclusions at the end of the first part of this essay and subsequently supported by a review of research in the American context. As a kind of overview as well as an indication of where coalition theory should go we will briefly review the work of Martin Levine (1971), as it is a good candidate for future development along the lines we have suggested.

Levine surmised that the consistent U-shaped roll-call distributions observed in American legislatures actually represented a bi-modal distribution with each mode representing a particular kind of situation. Using roll-data from the United States Senate he found that there are in fact two broad sets of roll-calls—those that are bargaining and those that are not. Those motions on which some bargaining takes place will be distributed around a mode toward the minimal end of the opposition continuum; those that do not involve bargaining will be distributed around a mode close to unanimity (see Figure 15). Levine also found that he could predict which issues would tend to produce bargaining thus supporting the earlier conclusion that issue content is an important variable in coalition formation. Also, in attempting to explain the entire range of coalition sizes he is pursuing another of our recommendations.

The manner in which Levine attempts to explain coalition formation is conceptually distinct from most of the models considered elsewhere. Rejecting the contingency assumption implicit in the n-person game conceptualization, he assumes that coalition builders will bring people into the competing coalitions through direct side-payment purchase of their support rather than by offering a proportional share of the winning outcome. This means

(1) the bargaining does not represent a game situation but instead simply an opportunity to sell a valued commodity to the higher of two bidders,

(2) the payoff for a particular winning coalition need not be divisible since it is not the source of the side-payments,

(3) the bargaining situation is essentially reduced from an n-person one to a two-person one,

(4) the payoff for most legislators is contingent upon the positions they take rather than whether or not they are in the winning coalition, and

(5) while the conflict between the coalition builders *may* approach zero-sum, for all of the nonplayers in the legislature who receive payoffs simply for voting with one side or the other the process is in no way zero-sum.

One key assumption is that while some legislators will be free agents in the manner described above, many will already have a disposition to vote one way or another depending on prior attitudes or pressures external to the legislature. It is this factor which keeps the side-payment total within reason and which also helps explain the larger than minimum coalitions. On some issues the predispositions are such that there is little controversy and thus no reason to bargain. On others the predispositions are such that there is conflict and enough uncommitted members for coalition builders to bid for support. Levine postulates that in this case there is a normal tendency to avoid risk and thus build coalitions approaching one-half plus one of the entire house, although he distinguishes his position from Koehler's by noting that such behavior is to be found only on an identifiable subset of all motions rather than as an across-the-board tendency.

Levine does not mention one other set of conditions, although his model provides for the possibility. That is where an issue so arouses constituency opinion that the legislators take positions commensurate with their respective constituency preferences and the resulting distribution of roll-call positions produces a winning coalition that is between a majority of those voting and a majority of the entire house in size. This would be an instance where coalition builders are severely constrained by outside forces which leave few if any legislators open to side-payments.

What Levine has introduced implicitly is the notion of ideology or policy distance. He is saying, in effect, that there is no point in coalition builders offering side-payments to those who are unlikely to agree with a particular policy since side-payments would be exeeptionally high, if effective at all. Also, on some issues the ideological content is such as to hamstring legislative bargaining because of the policy preference distribution among the public at large. Thus, Levine's model is commensurate with the recommendations we made earlier. Furthermore, his model implies that what constitutes rational behavior will vary from time to time depending on conditions. If rational behavior is defined as choosing more over less, then the actor will respond in such a way that his behavior will maximize the total payoff with respect to the goals relevant to a particular issue. On one occasion there may be no outside pressures threatening his receiving continued support from an important set of his constituents and no ideological preferences so that he can concentrate on maximizing the side-payments he receives. On another occasion he must ignore side-payments and concentrate on preserving his political support; and at another time he may respond to his own strong inclinations or preferences to maximize some psychological satisfaction. Of course he will often face situations where competing goals must be balanced. Initial research indicates that there are regularities in the manner in which legislators respond to different types of issues, and future research should focus on relating goals to issue content and to behavior patterns. One strength of Levine's model is that it leaves open for now the question of what goals are to be assumed, although he assumes there will be a cluster of goals and not just one.

CONCLUSION

Minimum coalition theories have proven to be of little use in ordering legislative data, if for no other reason than minimum-sized winning coalitions are relatively infrequent. However, in testing various minimum coalition theories, both in the parliamentary context and in the American legislative context, political scientists have reached basically similar conclusions as to how these theories need to be modified.

We have suggested that until recently theories of coalition formation have suffered in their data-ordering capabilities because their assumptions effectively masked important sources of variance. Empirical research in coalition formation has gradually resulted in these assumptions being lifted in favor of additional independent variables. With a closer examination of rationality the cycle will be essentially complete.

Even when this cycle is completed we will still be a long way from a complete theory of coalition formation in legislatures. A great deal of theoretical work will remain to rigorously determine whether the predictions which match observed behavior do in fact flow logically from the new models being developed.

It is possible, however, to summarize the general outlines of an empirically productive model of coalition formation based upon results already obtained. Any useful theory of coalition formation will need to display at least the following characteristics if it is to be applied in the legislative context:

(1) It will need to account for the entire range of coalition sizes and not just those of minimum size.

(2) It will need to be a spatial model which does not assume a zero-sum situation.

(3) It will need to assume seriality—each coalition is only one behavioral time slice in an ongoing process—rather than assuming every coalition is an independent phenomenon.

(4) It should probably avoid assuming perfect information.

(5) It should include policy distance as an important variable, and may need to include ideology as a particular source of policy distance with special impact.

(6) It should include issue content as an important variable.

(7) It should leave some room for the impact of prior factional alignments which will vary from house to house and often from session to session.

(8) It should define payoffs in such a way that it includes nondivisible as well as divisible forms and thus take into account the symbolic content of legislation.

(9) No matter how rationality is defined goals should be viewed as multiple rather than singular so that as the various conditions listed above shift, the relationship between the various goals will shift resulting in alternative predictions for coalition behavior.

This last characteristic suggests only that behavior shifts as conditions change. It does not require a multiple definition of rationality, nor does it imply that rationality be dropped as an assumption.

These nine points are recommendations for the general content of future coalition theory. Our basic recommendation for approaching the study of coalitions in the near future is to shift from an assumption of substantive rationality to one of procedural rationality and to pursue this approach partly by interviewing legislators directly as to their goal orientations.

NOTES

1. It is not clear whether Riker intended his model to be applied to the study of legislative coalition building. Some have argued that attacking the utility of his theory in such a context is to take on a straw man. However, regardless of his intent, students of coalition formation have almost always considered his model a candidate for ordering legislative data. See Axelrod (1970), Browne (1973), Damgaard (1972), Francis (1970), Hinckley (1972), Koehler (1972a, 1972b, 1971), and Leiserson (1970, 1968) for just a few examples. Thus, in our critique we are not so much attacking Riker as we are questioning consistent use of his model by others in the legislative context.

2. There is one more effort that should be noted, although an unfortunate definitional problem prevents it from being evidence of any kind for our purposes. Lawrence C. Dodd (1974) establishes that minimum sized coalitions in the European parliamentary context are more "durable." He suggests this is support for Riker's theorem, but unfortunately Dodd's definition of minimum coalition is such as to prove little. In this study a minimum winning coalition is one which "(1) has a reliable majority, yet (2) contains no party in the coalition that is unnecessary to majority status." Readers will recognize this as similar to a definition originally advanced by Michael Leiserson—a definition which research has indicated neither predicts the same coalitions as Riker's nor is any more successful at accurate predictions than Riker's. For example, looking at the hypothetical parliamentary situation outlined in the body of this essay, the following coalitions would meet Dodd's definition as minimal and winning—BC (41 seats), CE (37 seats), ABDE (37 seats), CDF (33 seats), and ABEF (34 seats). Obviously his definition permits a wide range of sizes to be called minimal which not only vitiates prediction but cannot really provide support for Riker's theory, which would require minimal to be 33 seats or very close to that figure. Dodd reaches an interesting conclusion but his definition is so broad that almost any of the competing models can claim support for their position from his results. Thus his effort is neither consistent nor inconsistent with our conclusions.

3. As is clear from Figure 14, the 1961 House session had many more roll-calls of every size. It had twice as many roll-calls as any other session of either house and twice as many minimal (closely divided) roll-calls as any other session. Specific comparative figures are provided in Table 2.

TABLE 2
Texas Legislative Voting Data[a]

Session	Average Percent in Winning Coalition	Number of Minimal Votes	Percent Minimal Votes
1961 House	65.5	181	27.0
1963 House	64.5	88	39.2
1965 House	67.5	53	14.4
1967 House	67.5	91	16.7
1969 House	70.0	79	15.1
1961 Senate	68.7	58	17.3
1965 Senate	68.9	30	12.7
1969 Senate	68.9	48	19.0
All Sessions	68.0	628	19.2

[a] Reproduced from Lutz and Murray.

4. While the large number of closely divided roll-calls does not explain the prominent mode, there probably is a connection between the two phenomena. The 1961 session of the Texas House was a case of prior factional alignment producing a new, not altogether firm coalition of liberals and moderates comprising a little over a majority of the entire House. As we argue below, on a large number of issues this coalition held firm and this explains the prominent mode. On those issues where it was apparent from debate and back hall discussion that the coalition would hold, those in the minority had little incentive to vote to the contrary unless for symbolic reasons—since to do so was to cross the speaker needlessly. Thus, on those roll-calls where a majority of the House held firm we would expect the vote not to be close—which is what we tend to find. However, whenever it became apparent to the minority coalition leaders that the majority coalition had cracks, they marshalled their forces and bargained with the less committed members of the majority coalition with considerable success. Thus, the large number of closely divided roll-calls with the winning majority in the 60 to 70 range is indicative of the instability of the coalition behind the speaker. That is, if the majority coalition which elected the speaker and wrote the rules had been larger and/or more stable there would have been far fewer closely divided roll-calls. The uniqueness of the 1961 session is, therefore, probably summarized in these two aggregate voting patterns.

5. We are thankful to Martin Levine for pointing out this formulation of the findings. It is interesting that the conclusions reached by Lutz and Murray are quite similar to those reached by the more "traditional" literature on American legislatures. For example, Warren E. Miller and Donald E. Stokes (1963) demonstrated over a decade ago that the relationship between a congressman and his constituency will vary according to the issue involved. Furthermore they concluded that of the three policy areas they studied the one which most conformed to the instructed-delegate model of the representation (that is, where the legislator was responding primarily to his constituency) was civil rights legislation. This is precisely the kind of issue on which Lutz and Murray surmise that Texas legislators were responding to their constituencies as it had a high symbolic content.

6. We do not mean that if goals were known we could not determine coalition size. Rather, we mean that there is no way to determine a priori what goals are being pursued, and the coalition building process will vary as the goals being pursued vary. An interesting corollary to this point is one made by Steven J. Brams and John G. Heilman several years ago (1971). They argue, in a theoretical paper, that what constitutes rational behavior will also vary according to the expectations of the participants as to what the probable or most likely outcome will be. If a participant is uncommitted and expects a minimum winning coalition, one form of behavior is most rational; while if he expects a larger than minimum winning coalition, another kind of behavior is rational.

7. Paul T. Hill has proposed that we treat rationality as a variable (1973: 14). However, he fails to follow his own advice and in the model he builds he assumes a rationality defined by a singular behavior. On the other hand, Hill does distinguish between two broad categories which, in effect, account for some variance in behavior based on differential weighting of goals. The first category includes those situations where both satisfaction and payoff can be maximized by the same coalition behavior. Policy satisfaction is so defined that it could include consideration of constituency pressure as well as psychological satisfaction associated with meeting ideological preferences. The second category includes those coalition situations where a legislator must choose between maximizing policy satisfaction or payoff

since behavior aggrandizing one will diminish the other. Hill's distinction is a useful one for moving coalition theory in the direction we have recommended.

8. Allan Mazur (1968) provides one interesting example of a "nonrational" approach. He is typical of such theorists in that he rejects a crude, narrow definition of rationality which requires actors to maximize a single, measurable utility. Using anthropological data he finds that tribal coalition builders apparently act to preserve balance and identity-consistency. This must be considered rational in at least a minimal sense since this matching of coalition behavior to specific goals is purposive and not random; such behavior would be considered rational under the stricter definition we suggest, using maximizing behavior over multiple goals, some of which are not measurable in the strict sense of the word.

A more interesting proposal is one made by Herbert A. Simon (1957). He argues that some behavior which appears irrational is in fact a rational response to the limited information-processing, reasoning, and computing ability of the human brain; that the traditional assumption of maximizing behavior should be replaced by an assumption of "satisficing" behavior. Riker and Ordeshook (1973), on the other hand, argue in the second chapter of their book that there is no essential difference in the behavior which results from satisficing and behavior which results from maximizing.

The entire matter of rationality is a complex one and a theoretical discussion of the concept lies outside the purpose of this essay. Any serious thinking about the meaning and implications of rationality for political behavior will have to face a whole series of theoretical problems some of which are nicely set forth by Nigel Howard (1971).

9. There is at least one attempt to do just this in an empirical test of Riker's theory, although it is not concerned with legislative coalitions. Marjorie Randon Hershey (1973) interviewed 28 congressional candidates and 29 campaign managers to determine whether they aimed at gaining a minimum winning coalition among the voters or a "big victory." She discovered that the Wisconsin congressional campaigners responded differently from the predictions of Riker's analysis. While the analysis is somewhat involved, two points she makes is that there is more than one motivation at work and these multiple motivations interact as a result of contextual conditions—the most important of which is the nature of the party system. Since Riker himself argued that American elections fall into the category of n-person zero-sum games (Riker, 1962: 55), Hershey's findings must be considered provocative, although not conclusive. The consistent application of Riker's theory within the legislative context would seem to require a parallel research effort for the same reason that Hershey's research should be extended within the electoral context.

REFERENCES

ADRIAN, C. and C. PRESS (1968) "Decision costs in coalition formation." Amer. Pol. Sci. Rev. 62 (June): 556-563.

AXELROD, R. (1972) Conflict of Interest: A Theory of Divergent Goals with Applications to Politics. Chicago: Markham.

BICKER, W. E. (1969) "The Assembly Party: change and consistency in legislative voting behavior in the Indiana House, 1923-1963." Ph.D. dis. Indiana University.

BRAMS, S. J. and J. G. HEILMAN (1971) "When to join a coalition and with how many others, depends on what you expect the outcome to be." Paper presented at Annual Meeting of the Amer. Pol. Sci. Assn.

BROWNE, E. C. (1973) Coalition Theories: A Logical and Empirical Critique. Sage Prof. Papers in Comparative Politics, 1, 01-043. Beverly Hills and London: Sage.

BUTTERWORTH, R. L. (1971) "A research note on the size of winning coalitions." Amer. Pol. Sci. Rev. 65 (September): 741-745.

DAMGAARD, E. (1973) "Party coalitions in Danish law-making, 1953-1970." European J. of Pol. Research 1: 35-66.

——— (1972) "A coalitional approach to legislative politics: the case of Denmark." Paper presented at Annual Meeting of the Midwest Pol. Sci. Assn.

DeSWAAN, A. (1970) "An empirical model of coalition formation as an n-person game of policy distance minimization," in S. Groennings, E. W. Kelley, and M. Leiserson [eds.] The Study of Coalition Behavior: Theoretical Perspectives and Cases from Four Continents. New York: Holt, Rinehart & Winston.

DIESING, P. (1971) Patterns of Discovery in the Social Sciences. Aldine-Atherton.

DODD, L. C. (1974) "Party coalitions in multiparty parliaments: a game theoretical analysis." Amer. Pol. Sci. Rev. 68: forthcoming.

FLANAGAN, S. (1973) "Theory and method in the study of coalition formation." J. of Comparative Admin. 5 (November): 267-314.

FRANCIS, W. (1970) "Coalitions in American state legislatures," in S. Groennings, E. W. Kelley, and M. Leiserson [eds.] The Study of Coalition Behavior: Theoretical Perspectives and Cases from Four Continents. New York: Holt, Rinehart & Winston.

GAMSON, W. A. (1962) "Coalition formation at presidential nominating conventions." Amer. J. of Soc. 68 (September): 156-171.

——— (1961a) "A theory of coalition formation." Amer. Soc. Rev. 26: 373-382.

——— (1961b) "An experimental test of a theory of coalition formation." Amer. Soc. Rev. 26 (August): 565-573.

GROENNINGS, S., E. W. KELLEY and M. A. LEISERSON [eds.] (1970) The Study of Coalition Behavior: Theoretical Perspectives and Cases from Four Continents. New York: Holt, Rinehart & Winston.

HERSHEY, M. R. (1973) "Incumbency and the minimum winning coalition." Amer. J. of Pol. Sci. 17 (August): 631-637.

HILL, P. T. (1973) A Theory of Political Coalitions in Simple and Policy-Making Situations. Sage Prof. Papers in American Politics, 1, 04-008. Beverly Hills and London: Sage.

HINCKLEY, B. (1972) "Coalitions in Congress: size and ideological distance." Midwest J. of Pol. Sci. 16 (May): 197-207.

HOWARD, N. (1971) The Paradoxes of Rationality: The Theory of Metagames and Political Behavior. Cambridge, Mass.: MIT Press.

KARNS, D. A. (1974) "Legislative roll-call analysis: the individual differences scaling approach." Paper presented at Annual Meeting of the Midwest Pol. Sci. Assn.

KOEHLER, D. (1972a) "The legislative process and the minimal winning coalition," in R. G. Niemi and H. F. Weisberg [eds.] Probability Models of Collective Decision Making. Columbus, Ohio: Merrill.

——— (1972b) "Coalition formation in selected state legislatures." Paper presented at Annual Meeting of the Midwest Pol. Sci. Assn.

——— (1971) "Coalition formation and the legislative process." Paper presented at Annual Meeting of the Amer. Pol. Sci. Assn.

LeBLANC, H. (1969) "Voting in state senates: party and constituency influences." Midwest J. of Pol. Sci. 13 (February): 33-57.

LEISERSON, M.A. (1970) "Power and ideology in coalition behavior," in S. Groennings, E. W. Kelley, and M. A. Leiserson [eds.] The Study of Coalition Behavior: Theoretical Perspectives and Cases from Four Continents. New York: Holt, Rinehart & Winston.

––– (1968) "Factions and coalitions in one-party Japan." Amer. Pol. Sci. Rev. 62 (September): 770-787.

––– (1966) "Coalitions in politics: a theoretical and empirical study." Ph.D. dis. Yale University.

LEVINE, M. D. (1971) "Coalition formation in the United States Senate." Paper presented at Annual Meeting of the Midwest Pol. Sci. Assn.

LUTZ, D. S. and R. W. MURRAY (forthcoming) "Issues and coalition size in the Texas Legislature: a further test of Riker's theory." Western Pol. Q.

MAZUR, A. (1968) "A nonrational approach to theories of conflict and coalitions." J. of Conflict Resolution 12 (June): 196-205.

McCALLY, S. (1966) "The governor and his legislative party." Amer. Pol. Sci. Rev. 60 (December): 923-942.

MILLER, W. E. and D. E. STOKES (1963) "Constituency influence in Congress." Amer. Pol. Sci. Rev. 57 (March): 45-56.

MOORE, D. W. (1969) "Legislative effectiveness and majority party size: a test in the Indiana House." J. of Politics 31 (November): 1063-1079.

MURRAY, R. W. and E. S. LUTZ (1974) "Redistricting in the American states: a test of the minimal winning coalition hypothesis." Amer. J. of Politics 18 (May): 233-255.

NIEMI, R. G. and H. F. WEISBERG (1972) Probability Models of Collective Decision Making. Columbus, Ohio: Merrill.

RIKER, W. H. (1962) The Theory of Political Coalitions. New Haven: Yale Univ. Press.

––– and P. C. ORDESHOOK (1973) An Introduction to Positive Political Theory. Englewood Cliffs: Prentice-Hall.

TAYLOR, M. (1972) "On the theory of government coalition formation." Presented at a workshop on European cabinet coalitions, sponsored by the European Consortium for Political Research, Helvoirt, the Netherlands.

USLANER, E. M. (1974) "Partisanship and coalition formation in Congress." (mimeo).

––– (1973) "Conditions for party responsibility: partisanship in the House of Representatives: 1947-1970." Ph.D. dis. Indiana University.

DONALD S. LUTZ did undergraduate work at Georgetown University, earned his Ph.D. at Indiana University, and now teaches political science at the University of Houston. His articles have appeared in such publications as Journal of Politics, Western Political Quarterly, and Journal of Political Science; he is currently writing a book on the evolution of American political theory in the eighteenth century.

JAMES R. WILLIAMS, lecturer in political science at Texas A&M University, is a doctoral candidate at York University, Toronto. His dissertation research is in political psychology and political participation; his interests also include U.S. and Canadian politics, philosophy and techniques of social research, and political theory.

PREFACE

My interest in the subject of this study goes back several decades. It was rekindled a few years ago with the not inconsiderable interest in political development among social scientists. While their interest came about mainly because of the emergence of newly independent states in the wake of World War II, I was moved to do a type of case study of a state (Serbia) that was in the process of emerging from long years of colonial rule, and attempting to build its own political institutions, over a hundred years ago. What lessons there may be in this study for future scholarship dealing with political development or modernization is for others to judge.

I am especially grateful to the Earhart Foundation for generous assistance which has enabled me to pursue this study and to make the results a reality.

Alex N. Dragnich

Nashville, Tennessee
May 1978

TABLE OF CONTENTS

Table of Contents

I

INTRODUCTION

The mention of Serbia evokes among many readers the response "what is it?" or "where is it?" Even those who can answer these questions will, I hope, find the following brief historical notes helpful as an introduction to the chapters that follow. The first note deals with medieval Serbia, prior to her defeat by the Turks in 1389 and her extinction as a state in 1458 and her subsequent enslavement for some 400 years. The second is a brief survey of some essential factual data about Serbia in the nineteenth century. Following these is a brief statement concerning the objectives of this study and its relevance to the more general concerns of political science.

Serbia of the Middle Ages

Although many things are unknown about Serbia of the middle ages, we do know that for several centuries she occupied the heart of the Balkan peninsula, and for nearly a hundred years she was the principal power there. Travel routes across her linked east and west. Three famous Byzantine writers (Theodore Metohit, Nikifor Grigor and Jovan Kantakuzin) spent briefer or longer periods of time in Serbia, and their writings contain information about Serbian lands, people and state.[1]

The medieval Serbian state was organized on the monarchical principle, with the monarch usually having the title of tsar.[2] In addition, there were types of assemblies, and a number of writers have mentioned them, but much of what they have written is false or unauthoritative.[3] Too often there was a tendency to attribute to these assemblies more powers than the available evidence warrants. Most of the available evidence suggests that the members of assemblies came in the main from the nobility and the higher clergy. Although it was nowhere decreed as to who had a right to participate,[4] the assemblies at times appeared as broad national meetings. The monarch decided whom to call, and after receiving advice, he made the decisions, there being no evidence of debates. Understandably, the ruler used members of his family, his military cohorts, and others as more intimate advisors.[5]

The assemblies were called together to assist in the selection of the church head (patriarch), to hear proclamations from the ruler, or to witness his installation as monarch. Sometimes they were called together for advice on varied questions (concerning church government, determining administrative boundaries, proclamation of laws, determining areas of competence of government officials, etc.).[6]

The Serbian assemblies had a church-national character. At times they dealt with religious matters and at other times with state matters. Unlike in the West, the church in Serbia did not use the natural law doctrine as a way of seeking to limit the ruler and to put the church above the state. The Serbian clergy did not gather the nobility around itself as a way of limiting the monarch's authority, but as a way of becoming the ruler's strongest supporter and the guardian of national unity. Cooperation between church and state was felt in the Serbian state assemblies.[7]

With the beginning of the disintegration of the Serbian state (after Tsar Dušan's death in 1355), the possibility of holding assemblies became more difficult.[8] And with Serbia's defeat in 1389 and her subsequent extinction as a state, the assemblies came to an end. This was at the very time when they were tending to acquire a representative character, and when similar bodies were gaining an established place for themselves in western and central Europe.

The assemblies had helped, however, to create a sense of national identity which subsequently was to be perpetuated by the church. During the Turkish enslavement, the church continued to exist and to function, although in a more limited way. In a very real sense, some of the national attributes of the assemblies were taken over by the church. In this way, some scholars have maintained, the basis of the 19th century assemblies in Serbia can be traced back to the medieval Serbian state assemblies.[9]

It should also be noted that during the Turkish occupation the Serbs had some voice in local affairs. Serbia was divided into *nahije* or regions. These were ruled by Turkish governors who lived in the towns. Each *nahija* was divided into a number of principalities, and the latter were divided into peasant (communal) areas. Both principalities and communal areas (or peasant villages) had informal local assemblies which played some role in the control of local affairs. Many decisions concerning matters of general interest were reached following discussions in public meetings.[10]

On paper, the greatest political heritage of medieval Serbia is Tsar Dušan's Law Code.[11] This Code was an independent Serbian creation, although it may have borrowed or adapted certain rules from Byzantine law. The Code is a combination of public and private law, seeking to regularize and systematize social, economic, and political relations. It was probably made necessary as a way of recognizing the economic and social changes that had taken place. It was designed to protect the rights of peasants as well as the rights of the nobility. It included penalties, among other things, for homicide, arson, theft, drunkenness, swearing, bribery, and counterfeiting. It also laid down rules for judges and for the clergy.

When Serbia revolted against the Turks in 1804, and subsequently set about developing its own judicial institutions, it is not altogether clear what impact Dušan's Code had. It is known that Matija Nenadović, one of the most learned men of that time who was given the task of drafting laws, had a copy of Justinian's Code, and he was familiar with the Mosaic law. Although Nenadović does not mention Dušan's Code in his memoirs, some Serbian scholars insist that he borrowed more from Dušan's Code than from any other.[12]

In some ways the most impressive heritage of medieval Serbia, certainly the most physically visible, are the monasteries. At one time there were over twenty major ones and many minor ones. Despite centuries of neglect during the Turkish occupation, many of these are remarkably well-preserved, and testify in some degree to the cultural level which the Serbs had attained. Interestingly enough, the heritage which Serbian rulers passed on were monasteries and not castles (at least there is no evidence of the latter).

The monasteries were more than religious institutions; they were also cultural and educational centers. There is also some evidence that the monasteries were centers of economic life as well as being political centers.[13] The latter can be said at least about those monasteries that were heavily fortified. The building of some monasteries was probably politically motivated, as a way of tying the church and state together and thereby strengthening the latter.

The political importance of the monasteries in the period of Turkish rule is two-fold. First, they were and continued to be visible symbols of national identity. Secondly, they were places where in a limited way the clergy could get some education, and were thereby enabled to pass on in oral communication something of Serbia's historical and cultural heritage.

The idea of national identity was perpetuated in large measure by Serbian Orthodox priests. They conveyed to the people the idea that the Serbian nation had a religious mission, that it was difficult to think of a really free church without a truly independent country. The past glories of the Serbian nation were also perpetuated in a type of oral history and oral literature. In folk tales, songs, and legends, talented people passed on to new generations notions of past glory, the exploits of national heroes, and dreams of national resurrection. Moreover, many Serbs who lived abroad (e.g., in Montenegro, Austria, and Hungary) devoted their intellectual efforts toward the preservation of Serbian national identity and worked toward the realization of Serbian independence.

Few peoples celebrate the anniversary of their greatest defeat. Usually it is the great national victories or triumphs that are commemorated. But for the Serbs the defeat at Kosovo (1389) and the death there of Tsar Lazar has not been pictured as a defeat. Rather, it is depicted as a dedication on the part of those who fell at Kosovo to higher and more noble goals than the materialistic possessions of this world. Over the centuries, Kosovo became a propaganda symbol and more. It embodied the myth of one-time national greatness that helped people to survive and to look toward a better day. The Serbian state had taken such deep roots in the people that it continued to live in the spirit of the Serbs even when political independence had been lost. The Serbs had, in effect, assumed a solemn oath to avenge Kosovo.

In terms of social structure, the Serbia of the middle ages had developed into a type of fedual society. There were classes and there were privileged elements. It is important to note, however, that classes were not yet organized and that there were no class assemblies.[14] The ruler relied in the main on mercenaries, and granted special privileges to the nobility only where he was forced by circumstances to do so.

In any case, whatever feudalism had been established was destroyed by the long years of Turkish occupation. The Turks controlled all the towns and all Serbs became essentially peasants. When Serbia regained her independence in the 19th century there was no aristocracy or nobility. There were some more or less well-to-do peasants, but by and large the newly independent Serbia became a nation of small landholders. Thus Serbia was able to develop in the 19th century without feudalism and without clericalism. And Prince Miloš Obrenović, who was the recognized ruler of Serbia between 1815 and 1838, did not permit the establishment of a nobility.

The resurrected Serbian nation was a peasant society.[15] A number of factors helped to preserve its peasant character. First of all, the peasant had his own land. And the law did not permit the sale of his land, house or livestock (below a certain minimum) for the payment of debts. Seocndly, he was armed, which gave him a certain feeling of independence. Parenthetically, it might be noted that not until 1883 did a ruler dare to attempt to take the peasants' arms, an attempt that precipitated a serious rebellion. Thirdly, in one way or another the peasant was consulted about problems of common concern and thereby participated in the decisions. Aside from the ancient assemblies, mentioned earlier, there were various types of local or regional gatherings. Fourth, "family particularism" was strong. Men who left peasant areas to become merchants, craftsmen, and civil servants did not break with their relatives in the countryside. This was more than a tie with the land and the peasant village; it was a tie with relatives, with brothers.

All in all, the Serbs possessed an unusual national and historical awareness. They were of one religion, one national tradition, one way of life. In their hearts they carried the Kosovo myth. There were no big towns, no tribalism, no feudalism, and no large landholdings. And while people of other religions or nationalities were not numerous, the Serbs demonstrated a strong power of assimilation in the case of the non-Serbs who lived among them. Moreover, the people were not overawed by foreigners on their throne, for unlike in many other European nations, the Serbian monarchs were Serbs and not members of the great royal houses of Europe.

What can we conclude from what has been said above? First of all, for Serbian nation-building in the 19th century, the survival of a strong sense of national identity was the most important. Second in importance was a social structure that made for a sense of equality and common purpose. Finally, the historical experience of institutions (e.g., assemblies; clan and village meetings), which to a degree meant a primitive form of democratic decision-making, contributed to the early development of challenges to one-man rule.

Serbia in the 19th Century

After some 400 years of Turkish subjugation, the Serbs launched a successful revolution in 1804, but this was followed by almost incessant warfare until the Turks were able to reassert their rule in 1813. In 1815 there was a second successful uprising, which gradually brought autonomy to the Serbs, although it was not officially recognized until the Turkish hatisherif (a type of constitution for Serbia) of 1830. With these two uprisings, the Serbs began the process of rebuilding their state.

The geographic size of the Serbian state in its early years of resurrection can only be approximated. In 1815 it was about the size of the state of Massachusetts (less than 10,000 square miles). It was increased considerably by 1833, and following the wars against Turkey (1876-1878) it occupied an area of some 18,800 square miles (the combined size of Vermont and New Hampshire). As a result of the Balkan Wars (1912-1913), the area of Serbia increased to some 34,000 square miles (about the geographic area of the state of Maine).

In population, Serbia went from less than 500,000 in 1815 to nearly 1 million at mid-century. By 1890 the population exceeded 2 million, and by 1910 it was approaching 3 million. Following the Balkan Wars—on the eve of World War I—the population of Serbia was approximately 4.5 million, with the capital city (Belgrade) having close to 100,000 inhabitants. In 1850 Belgrade had fewer than 15,000, although fifty years earlier its population had been about 25,000.

During the period of long Ottoman rule, Serbs migrated in large numbers, mainly to Hungary and Austria. After 1804 and after 1815, many Serbs came back from these countries, and some came from Bosnia, Hercegovina, and Montenegro. Many were induced to come by grants of free land and exemption from taxes for periods up to three years. Those who came back from Austria were perhaps the most influential, because by and large they were the educated Serbs who became teachers, professors, engineers, and civil servants in the newly re-established state. While their services were invaluable, their presence and privileges were soon resented by many native aspirants to government offices.

On the whole, however, the population was homogeneous, especially as the Turks left the few towns which had primarily been their outposts. For most of the 19th century, over 90 per cent of the Serbs lived on the land, with small land holdings being the rule. As noted earlier, during the period of Ottoman rule the Turks had wiped out the nobility and aristocracy of medieval Serbia, and during a critical period after the second revolution (1815) the Serbian ruler (Miloš Obrenović) did not permit the establishment of a nobility. Moreover, in the new Serbia there were no big towns, no tribalism, no feudalism. and no regional animosities.

At the beginning of the 19th century Serbia was a rather primitive land.[16] By comparison with Western Europe there was general backwardness. There was little or no industry. Even in the largest center, Belgrade, glass windows and mirrors were rare, and in the interior they were unknown. No factory-made candles were available in any shop in Belgrade as late as 1841. Tables and chairs were non-existent even in the ruler's household except in his offices, and even he slept on the floor until 1834. Tableware was non-existent or scarce. Even in the so-called palace metal dishes and wooden spoons were used to eat from as late as 1834. Communications, except for some river-boat traffic, were virtually non-existent. There were a few primitive roads and trails which were used by those who had horses or oxen. How Serbia had retrogressed under Ottoman rule can be appreciated if one recalls that in most aspects of everyday life, the Serbia of the middle ages was no less advanced than Western European societies of that time.

The general cultural situation in Serbia at the outset of the 19th century was equally dismal. Literature had pretty well died out, and even the priests and monks were practically illiterate (the Church hierarchy was controlled by Greeks). Schools were rare, and even by 1836 there were no more than sixty schools and about as many teachers, most of them by birth from Austria and poorly trained. Books and paper were rare; the first bookstore was opened in 1827. The hatisherif of 1830 permitted the establishment of printing presses, as well as the building of hospitals. There were no hospitals in 1815, and no certified doctors until 1819. The first pharmacy was opened in 1826, and the first mention of a hospital came in 1832.

Serbia's socio-economic conditions did not change much in the early years of the 19th century, but the one saving grace was that throughout the century Serbia continued to be a nation of small landholders. Over 80 per cent of the holdings were under 25 acres, and over 95 per cent were under 50 acres.[17] Moreover, after 1833 the peasant had full control over the land he worked, and an 1873 law prevented the peasant from selling or in any other way disposing of a certain minimum (12 acres) of his holdings. This was designed to protect a portion of his holdings from being taken to satisfy tax defaults or debts.

Stock-raising, which had grown rapidly in the 18th century, was the predominant characteristic of the Serbian economy. In the 19th century land cultivation developed alongside stock-raising. The principal exports consisted of hogs, steers, sheep, wool, and hides. By the 1880s and 1890s, the three main articles of export were livestock (by all odds the largest), fruit (some fresh and some processed), and cereals, with 90 per cent of the exports going to Austria-Hungary. In the same period 90 per cent of Serbia's imports came from the Dual Monarchy. Austro-Hungarian pressures against Serbia in the early 1900s enabled the Serbs to establish important trade links elsewhere, mainly with Germany, but also with Belgium, France, Switzerland, and Britain. The peasants suffered, however, from shortages in farm implements and draft animals (oxen and horses).

The development of industry was slow, and for the most part took place late in the century. There were many reasons: lack of capital, lack of skilled manpower, poor communications connections (first railroads were built in the early 1880s), insufficient legal security, an unfavorable foreign trade position vis-à-vis the powerful industrially-developed neighbor, Austria-Hungary, and the failure of the Serbian government to assist in industrialization. Even the efforts of the Young Conservatives cabinet in 1873 to encourage industry, through various concessions (free timber, free use of land, assurance of monopoly control, exemptions from direct taxes and customs duties) did not result in much industrialization.

With the 1880s Serbia began to create the most necessary institutions needed for economic development. A beginning had been made in the 1870s with the creation of private financial institutions, which was speeded up in the 1880s. Moreover the 1880s saw the beginning of a series of trade agreements, loans, building of railroads, creation of a national bank, and the construction of public buildings and schools. As a dependent state, Serbia had been prevented from concluding her own foreign trade agreements until after the Treaty of Berlin (1878), which formally recognized her independence. Industrial enterprises increased in number in the 1890s and the early 1900s, yet no new railroads were constructed between 1885 and 1905.

The period 1903-1914, during which the Radical party was almost exclusively in power, saw considerable progress in the economic regeneration of the nation. Loans were secured after 1905 for the building of additional railroads and for modernizing the army, two areas that had been neglected. There was also a regeneration of Serbia's exports, leading toward her economic emancipation from Austria-Hungary. State expenditures rose in the 1905-1912 period from about 3.5 million to some 4.8 million £. Yet revenues also increased, so that government budgets showed a net surplus.[18]

As we look at 19th century developments in Serbia, one other factor needs to be kept in mind, even though it cannot be weighed at various points along the way. This involves external forces, i.e., the influence of the Great Powers of Europe. The rivalries of these powers and their fate over nearly six centuries in large measure determined the fate of the Serbs. In the 19th century, the Great Power rivalries centered in part on the outcome of the decaying Ottoman empire. The rivalry of Russia and Austria-Hungary was especially pronounced, but Great Britain was no less interested in developments in the Balkans and the eastern Mediterranean.[19] France and Germany, too, perceived that what happened in the Balkans could affect the balance of power in Europe. Consequently, Serbian rulers often found themselves pressured by the representatives of the Great Powers not only concerning Serbia's foreign policies, but also in matters of domestic politics. Therefore, one cannot lose sight of these important external factors if Serbian developments are to be reasonably understood.

Objectives of this Study

In the main, my aim in the chapters that follow is to depict and to explain the establishment and evolution of political institutions in 19th century and early 20th century Serbia. While the treatment is largely chronological, the main theme is the struggle for democracy, and particularly the drive to secure parliamentary government. The changes in political organization, the struggles for power, and ultimately the victory of parliamentary democracy are succinctly described. Finally, some effort is made to point to the factors that help to explain the evolution of Serbia's political institutions.

In a sense this is a case study of political development in historical perspective, from the uprising against the Turks in 1804 until Serbia became part of the new Yugoslav state in 1918. Because our political development literature has precious little in the way of historical case studies, it is my hope that this book will be a modest addition to this respect, and that it will assist in our quest for a better understanding of what we have come to call political development.

PART I. NATION-BUILDING

II
THE STRUGGLE FOR AUTONOMY, 1804-1838

The events associated with the Serbian uprisings (often referred to as revolutions) of 1804 and 1815 against the Turks can broadly be characterized as embodying struggles for autonomy (ultimately independence), and for the creation of a domestic political system. While the first was a prerequisite for the second, the second is more at the center of this book. In the course of the struggle for autonomy (1804-1838), there were determined contests over the nature of domestic political institutions to be established, as well as who would effectively control them. Two names are prominently associated with Serbia's struggle for autonomy—Karadjordje Petrović and Miloš Obrenović.

Karadjordje's Serbia, 1804-1813

The growing restlessness of the Serbs after centuries of Ottoman rule, coupled with the corruption and insubordination of Turkish officials, led to a successful revolution in 1804. The revolution was provoked when the Janissaries, who had become a sort of Praetorian Guard bent on acquiring personal privileges, killed the lawful Turkish governor in Belgrade in 1801 and imposed a reign of terror, thereby taking away from the Serbs the modest rights of local self-government that they had acquired in the last decade of the 18th century. The initial aim of the Serbian revolt was not against Turkish rule as such, but a determination to restore the privileges of home rule that the Janissary leaders had taken away. After they defeated the Janissaries in 1804, the Serbs in 1805 defeated the Turkish army that had been sent against them, forcing the Turks to concede a certain autonomy for Serbia. This was followed by a period of incessant warfare, which ended with the reassertion of Ottoman rule in 1813.

The leader of the Serbian uprising of 1804 was Karadjordje (Black George) Petrović. He was chosen in part because of his military experience in the Austrian *Freicorps* and in part because certain prominent Serbs did not dare put themselves at the head of the revolutionary movement. When it became apparent, soon after the revolt began, that political questions could not be avoided, several of the prominent Serbs, including district military commanders, were not happy with Karadjordje's making political decisions. Consequently, a two-fold challenge to Karadjordje's authority arose, one more or less informal and one more or less formal. The informal challenge was led by the district military commanders at annual assemblies *(skupštine)*, while the formal challenge took the form of an officially created Council.

The idea of the Council seems to have been suggested by the Russian foreign minister (Chartorisky) to two prominent Serbs who had come to Petrograd seeking Russian assistance against the Turks.[1] The Council was to consist of one representative from each of the 12 districts *(nahije)* of the Belgrade domain *(pašaluk)*. It was to have the supreme political power in the land, and would thereby limit Karadjordje, through whose reluctant concurrence the Council was established in 1805.

The Council's powers and functions, however, were not well-defined, and it was never really recognized as the supreme political authority. On the one hand, it came into conflict with Karadjordje's aspiration to be the supreme ruler, and on the other, the desires of local and district leaders to retain as much power for themselves. The decisive factor was Karadjordje; anytime that the Council came into conflict with him, his word was sufficient to frustrate its goals or actions.

The struggle for power between Karadjordje and the Council was made more complex by virtue of the fact that the struggle for autonomy had become a struggle for independence. With the latter objective in mind, it was necessary to think of establishing a legal-constitutional order. To this end, some of Karadjordje's opponents were successful in getting a Russian representative (Konstantin K. Rodofinikin) to come to Serbia, avowedly to help the Serbs set up an orderly administration. He drafted a constitution which would limit Karadjordje's power. Karadjordje accepted the draft because he needed Russia's military assistance, and because he believed that his powers would not be limited in practice.[2]

The Rodofinikin draft was never implemented because it did not receive the required assent of the Russian tsar and that of a Serbian assembly. In its place, Karadjordje and his followers produced an octroyed constitution in December 1810. By this document, all Serbian military and civil leaders recognized Karadjordje (as well as his lawful descendants) as the supreme leader, to whom all pledged loyalty and allegiance. For his part, Karadjordje promised to exert a fatherly concern for his people, and to recognize the new Council as the supreme court of the land. Moreover, he agreed to issue all orders through the Council and in agreement with it.

In practical terms the new constitution gave nearly all power to Karadjordje, while the Council became the administrator of his commands. He was obligated to hear the Council's views but not to accept them. The distrust that continued between the two, and the resumption of the war against Turkey, made this constitution for the most part a dead letter. Despite some political setbacks which Karadjordje suffered in 1810, he was able to reassert his unquestionable power by January 1811.

The new constitutional acts of January 1811 confirmed Karadjordje's supremacy and made of the Council a type of central government, into which Karadjordje not only brought some of his strongest supporters, but also many of his opponents. One part of the Council became the first Serbian ministry, consisting of six ministers, while the other part of the Council became the supreme court. Together they constituted a type of central authority, exercising legislative power. Karadjordje was its president. In effect, therefore, the Council (ministers and judges) became Karadjordje's agent and servant.

In the struggle with his opponents, Karadjordje had certain advantages. Although he was self-willed and temperamental, his opponents behaved no better in their respective districts. His authoritarianism had the saving grace of representing unity in contrast with the separatism of his political foes. Moreover, the exigencies of war played into his hands. In addition, he placed a number of his actual or potential opponents in subordinate positions, thus separating them from their natural constituencies as well as diluting their powers.

Karadjordje's supremacy was, however, short-lived. Although in the Peace of Bucharest of 1812, Turkey recognized autonomy for Serbia, in 1813 she resumed her military operations against Serbia and succeeded in re-establishing her control. Consequently, the Serbian political structure that had evolved did not have an opportunity to prove itself.

Miloš' Serbia, 1815-1838

By 1815, the Turkish political terror in Serbian areas was at its height.[3] Following the restoration of Turkish power in 1813 and

Karadjordje's flight from Serbia, the Turks employed brutal means in an effort to teach the Serbs a lesson, i.e., that rebellion does not pay. The situation had become so bad by 1815 that leading Serbs were willing to risk everything in an effort to overthrow the Turkish yoke. The revolt was a success, in part because of Russia's intervention, which was made possible by the defeat of Napoleon. Turkey promised an autonomous administration for Serbia, but this promise was not to be fulfilled for years to come.

Miloš Obrenović, one of the leaders under Karadjordje, who was chosen to lead the revolt in 1815 at the age of 32, soon realized that it was unrealistic to seek full independence. In stressing his loyalty to the Porte, he made it known that what the Serbs wanted in Belgrade was a decent Turkish governor. More precisely, they wanted Marašli-Ali-paša. In the end, the Turks appointed him and left the matter of Serbian internal affairs to be worked out between Miloš and Marašli-Ali-paša. The agreement reached by the two became the basis for the management of Serbian internal affairs.

The system of Turkish rule remained. The Serbs, however, made the following modest gains: (1) the collection of taxes was transferred from Turkish to Serbian authorities, (2) a Serbian knez (local leader) was to take part in court cases involving Serbs, (3) the sum of money for the support of the Turkish governor and his entourage would be determined in agreement with national leaders, (4) a council of national leaders (knezes) would be established in Belgrade.[4] The Serbs thus gained something less than autonomy over a territory roughly half the size of Karadjordje's Serbia.

As the leader of the Serbs, Miloš faced two major tasks—to work for Serbian independence and to create a system of national political authority. In seeking these objectives, he worked on two fronts—the Turkish and the domestic. On the former, national survival was at stake, and on the latter, his personal survival would be determined. For Miloš, in the main, national survival and his personal survival were one and the same thing.

National survival required the nurturing of a precarious identity and working toward increased autonomy, especially in domestic affairs. This necessitated seeking Russian help and counsel while at the same time seeking to assure the Turks of continued Serbian loyalty. To perform this delicate and complicated task, Miloš was sure that he was the only one for the job. Threats to his leadership, therefore, were threats to national survival.

How Miloš sought to achieve his basic objectives is a long and intricate story.[5] What follows is but an effort to deal briefly with what appear to the author as the major elements in the picture—the struggle with the Turks for greater autonomy, as well as expansion of the national territories, and the struggle with domestic elements to secure Miloš's personal authority.

The situation created by the Marašli-Miloš agreement could not survive long in practice. Alongside Turkish authority, Serbian authority grew step by step, and ultimately replaced Turkish control. Turkey's desire for peace in Serbia, a condition that would deny to Russia a pretext for seeking fulfillment of the Bucharest agreement, contributed to the takeover. Moreover, Marašli-Ali had intended to disarm the populace after his agreement with Miloš. But it was soon evident to him that the people could not be disarmed without a serious struggle, and he did not dare to embark on that course.[6]

Moreover, Serbian authority began to displace the Turkish, partly because Turkish control was not so strong as it appeared. The financial resources of the Turkish governor in Belgrade (Marašli-Ali) were insufficient, particularly since he had learned to live in relative luxury. Miloš readily helped him, and as he became more and more financially dependent on Miloš, he had to tolerate the latter's efforts to substitute Serbian authority for Turkish.[7] Lesser Turkish officials were in even more desperate straits, and readily sold themselves to Miloš.[8] In short, Miloš used money to buy political control.

It might be added, parenthetically, that Miloš seems to have had a talent for war and politics. He knew how to handle the sword as well as the purse. He was to use a combination of these tactics at a later date (1830 and 1833) to get the Turks to recognize him as hereditary prince of Serbia (with dynastic rights for his male heirs), and to add six additional districts to the area of the nation.

Miloš initially expanded Serbian authority by ordering Serbian knezes to begin to perform judicial functions in their respective areas in cases involving Serbs.[9] Miloš also sought to improve justice by asking judges to use custom and sound reason in reaching their verdicts. In addition, he ordered judges to go to church on Sunday and on national holidays, and to fast on Wednesdays and Fridays. And he told them to spend more of their time in court rooms and less in coffee houses.[10]

Gradually, Miloš succeeded in transforming administrative (as well as judicial) authority to national elders who were in fact his bureaucrats, since he appointed them. In this way he became an all-powerful ruler in domestic affairs just as the Turkish governor had been before him.[11] There was much talk about assemblies (skupštine) of elders, but these limited Miloš's authority only to the extent that he wanted or permitted.[12] The members of the assemblies were picked by Miloš's civil servants. They met for a day or two when Miloš wanted it. From time to time, however, he felt the need of calling such assemblies to explain his policies and actions.

The Nature of Miloš's Authority

Miloš became an all-powerful ruler, but he rejected the charge that he wanted all authority in his hands. Hearing history read, he said, convinced him that strong rule was the best government when one people "is raising itself up from the ruins."[13] He viewed the people as children and he as their father, likening his power to that of parental authority over minors. He believed people to be vacillating, unreliable, and easily misled by promises. When angry, he referred to the people as an "unthankful bitch" and as "livestock without tails."[14]

Generally speaking, the people were not hostile toward Miloš until late in his regime. They knew from experience that it was possible to go from bad to worse. Turkish rule, Karadjordje's rule, and wars were for them a school of patience. Although not having some higher or wider concept of the state, the people seemed to have instinctively felt a need for harmony and unity, patiently bearing oppression and distress. Even elders in the society were willing to wait until Miloš had accomplished his basic tasks, and only then to seek security from his arbitrariness.

Early in his regime, Miloš gained the upper hand in relation to other leaders in the country. Before too much time was to pass, he was either appointing district elders or he was placing other men over them so as to reduce their status to that of ordinary bureaucrats. By the end of 1820, the main elders were mostly his brothers, other relatives, or friends.[15] Pursuant to the Marašli-Miloš agreement, the Serbs were allowed to have an office of their own in Belgrade. This was called the National Chancellery (*Narodna Kancelarija*), which was supposed to be the supreme Serbian administrative and judicial organ, made up of 12 knezes. But Miloš did not want the National Chancellery to become a governing body. And he did not allow it to become a representative body. It became his personal chancellery, and it went with him wherever he travelled. Through his secretaries, Miloš gave orders and made decisions from which there was no appeal.[16]

Miloš's authority was crude and primitive, but it was authority. He seems to have felt that power had to be made visible concretely in the form of a despot before the people could later view it abstractly, independent of the personal wielders of power. This concept probably could have been tolerated until about 1830. What Miloš seems to have failed to comprehend was the need to organize and systematize power. Any such effort, any written laws even, he viewed as a diminution of his power.

Miloš was ruthless with his enemies. His fear of domestic opposition resulted in the death of many of his opponents, real or imagined.[17] "Miloš killed so as not to be killed. In those crimes he saw only preventive measures for his security and the security of his personal interests, which he identified with national interests."[18] He even had Karadjordje killed in 1817 when he returned to Serbia in an alleged conspiracy against Miloš.[19] Not until 1835 did Miloš finally recognize Karadjordje's merits, approving a pension for his widow. Some twenty-five years later he was to refer to Karadjordje as a great hero in the new Serbian history.

Miloš's terror may have been greater and more cruel than that found in some new mid-twentieth century states, but there were few or no newsmen, or radio or television correspondents to tell about it. Miloš knew of many misdeeds committed by his subordinates, and sometimes he took energetic measures against some of the elders, but more often he had to ignore their misdeeds because politically he could not do without such men.

In addition to his personal enemies, Miloš had to deal with the outlaws. The large mass of outlaws took on the appearance of a national illness. This could be explained in part as a reaction against taxes and autocratic rule. More important perhaps is the fact that many people from various areas had moved into the Belgrade region because it was relatively secure. These were people who were primarily engaged in stock-raising and who had been involved in trouble elsewhere. They had a nomadic and anarchistic character. They had not lived under any systematic state authority, and found it difficult to adjust to the order and control of an organized state. The problem of the outlaws was not solved through administrative reforms or liberal policies, but by strong and raw repression—by sword and fire. Merciless and barbaric methods were employed, even against families of outlaws. But by 1826, the outlaws were virtually eliminated.

Being overwhelmed by all sorts of problems, Miloš sought men of utmost loyalty and devotion. They had to carry out his orders blindly. They had to catch outlaws and other criminals, to hang them, to beat them to death, or to torture them. Men of a genial disposition could not have survived in Miloš's service. The first of his officials were men with a suspicious past and generally adventurers.[20] In the primitive organization of the state, such men begin as the ruler's servants and helpers who carry out his orders. Then they become his officials and ministers. Along with all their faults, they were men who dreamed of a resurrected Serbian nation. But they lacked the necessary training for the business of advising and helping Miloš to organize Serbia politically.

Miloš was aware of the type of men around him, but he apparently felt helpless. Sometimes he cursed them out unmercifully and ordered some of them beaten. At the same time, he was suspicious of everyone, even his closest officials. He opened their mail and looked through their things.[21] On the whole, however, they served him well. And they were not bound by bureaucratic inertia for the simple reason that there were no established bureaucratic procedures to act as a brake on their actions.

Miloš's Achievements, the Decline of His Authority, and the Victory of His Opponents

First among Miloš's important achievements was his success in getting the Turks in 1830 to recognize him as hereditary prince of Serbia. Earlier (in 1817 and 1826), he had been declared hereditary prince by Serbian assemblies (skupštine) whose members he picked and controlled. Because he had succeeded in taking over supreme authority, Miloš got the Porte to give legal form to an already existing situation.[22] While this success was viewed by many as a selfish act, and even if it should be so considered, it was a great leap forward for the Serbian nation. In recognizing the hereditary principle, the Turks were saying that future monarchs of Serbia would come to power as a matter of right, thus giving up their power to pass on their acceptability.

Secondly, Miloš succeeded in 1833 in enlarging the Serbian state by gaining six additional districts, nearly doubling the size of the nation.[23] As in the case of the hereditary principle, Miloš raised the territorial issue. As a matter of fact, he raised both issues at a time when their realization seemed impossible. In each case, he had the diplomatic support of Russia, although in the final stages of gaining the six additional districts he used armed force and without any prior approval from the Porte. Russian support for the hereditary principle was hesitant, and not until Miloš's power was limited by the Council (discussed below) in 1838 did Russia formally lend its approval.[24]

Thirdly, Miloš was successful in establishing order in a fairly primitive society. His methods against the outlaws were brutal and gruesome, but he did establish respect for (and fear of) authority. And who is to say that it could have been done by more moderate means?

Finally, although he became extremely wealthy, Miloš prevented the rise of a landed aristocracy.[25] In the 1830s, he refused to reward his associates and friends with lands that were vacated by the Turks.[26] Instead, he divided the land among the peasants. This alienated his erstwhile friends and supporters, who began systematically to undermine his authority.

With his domestic policies, however, Miloš was unable to satisfy the basic wishes and needs of the most eminent men or those of the masses.[27] He had given the peasants land, but they were not sure that he would not take it away. Similarly, the civil servants were insecure. The people generally tolerated his arbitrariness for some fifteen years. They realized that Miloš was building a common house, but once it was built they wanted a voice in how the household would be run. Miloš did not agree. After that it was only a matter of time before he would have to go.

Opposition to Miloš's absolutism assumed serious proportions in the 1830s. His early rivals were liquidated by 1817, but important evidence of dissatisfaction with his rule was manifest in the 1820s.[28] Following the Djakovo rebellion in 1825, Miloš promised the setting up of a Council of State, which he established in 1826.[29] While in theory it was to concern itself with domestic and foreign affairs, Miloš exercised a veto power over all of its acts and, in effect, did not allow it to function. Miloš's opposition in the 1830s consisted mainly of his one-time associates who had risen to positions of power with him.

Throughout the 1830s, Miloš's rivals sought to undermine his authority with the people, and intrigued against him with the Porte. The hatisherif of 1830, which is often referred to as Serbia's first constitution, was a Turkish granted document. It created a Council of national leaders who would be appointed by the prince but would be irremovable. Moreover, it asserted that the prince should rule in agreement with the Council. But Miloš succeeded in ignoring that part of the hatisherif which provided for the Council.[30] In January, 1835, however, some of the more prominent popular leaders, along with several thousand men, met in Kragujevac to demand a constitution of Miloš.[31] The uprising was bloodless, and Miloš promised a constitution, which was adopted in February, 1835 by an assembly of four thousand participants.[32]

The constitution of 1835 was a democratic document, but it never really went into effect, for it was abolished one month after its promulgation. Miloš was only too happy to abolish it, but the chief reason for its demise was the intervention of Russia, Turkey, and Austria.[33] Nicholas I and Metternich were sworn enemies of constitutionalism irrespective of its character. This constitution was rendered especially offensive to them by its origin in a popular movement resembling a revolution. Turkey wanted no more independence for Serbia than was necessary, and welcomed the opportunity to mix in Serbian internal affairs. And Miloš welcomed the intervention because he did not wish to see his power limited by the Council or a parliament.

Following the abolition of the 1835 constitution, Serbia was really without a constitution until 1838. In those years, Miloš's rivals were becoming the favorites of the Porte. At the same time, Miloš prepared one constitutional project after another, only to have it rejected by Russia.[34] Other constitutional projects, suggested by foreign powers, were not to Miloš's liking. Not really wanting a constitution, Miloš was prepared to accept one only if it gave him the preponderance of power. But the constitution that was forced on Serbia in 1838, by means of another Turkish hatisherif, was far from being such a constitution.

The constitution was not a long or complete document, but it laid the foundations for twenty years of Serbia's political and governmental life. It divided power between the prince and the Council, but in reality the latter was superior. The Council was to consist of 17 members, one from each of seventeen districts, chosen from among the leading men of the respective districts. Most important, they could not be removed except with the consent of the Porte. In short, the Council could defy the prince with impunity so long as it had the confidence of the Porte.

Moreover, the constitution of 1838 destroyed the *National Skupština* which had been given considerable power by the constitution of 1835.[35] The Council did not want the Skupština which might interfere in its work. And the Porte did not desire an assembly, because it was much easier to influence the Council than the Skupština. It has been said that the constitution of 1838 divided power between the prince and the Council in such a manner that the Porte could influence the outcome by siding with one or the other party.

Miloš realized that he was shorn of any significant powers, and declared that he could not rule in conjunction with seventeen councillors who would be the organs of the Sultan.[36] Among other things, the prince had to choose his ministers from the Council, and if he dismissed them or they resigned, they went back to the Council. Not only were Council members irremovable, but in addition, new appointments to the Council could be made only upon recommendation of the Council. In this way, the Council became a self-perpetuating oligarchy. When Miloš suggested changes in the constitution, the members of the Council were opposed, styling themselves as *Ustavo-branitelji* (Defenders of the Constitution), i.e., the defenders of the constitution of 1838.

Miloš fled Serbia in April 1839, but he was back the same month, in part because of the urgings of the Russian Consul in Belgrade.[37] He had some information that certain army units, which were hostile to the Council, were on the move toward Belgrade. Apparently, he thought this show of support unnecessary because he sought, unsuccessfully, to discourage them.[38] Toma Vučić Perišić (usually known simply as Vučić), perhaps the most important leader of the Defenders of the Constitution, met these units with armed force and disarmed them. In this he had Miloš's support, but Vučić soon turned his newly-won power toward forcing Miloš to abdicate, which he did in June 1839.[39]

Following Miloš's abdication in 1839, his son Milan became prince but he was on his deathbed and it is doubtful if he ever realized that he was prince of Serbia. Thereupon the second son, Mihailo, became prince, but not for long. By 1842, the Defenders of the Constitution succeeded in driving the Obrenovićes from the throne, and in choosing Alexander Karadjordjević, the son of Karadjordje, as prince of Serbia. This indicated a complete victory for the oligarchical Council, for now the Obrenovićes were out and the new prince owed everything to the Council, by whose constitution he was willing to be limited. Although styling themselves as Defenders of the Constitution, the members of the Council transgressed against it insofar as they overthrew a dynasty which according to that very constitution had a hereditary right to the throne.[40]

RUDIMENTARY MODERNIZATION AND OLIGARCHIC RULE
1838-1858

After the ouster of Prince Miloš, the oligarchy (Defenders of the Constitution) needed some three years to consolidate their regime, which was to stay in power until 1858.[1] Secure in their positions on the Council, they initially set up a regency for Miloš's minor son, Mihailo, but subsequently forced him from the throne, and chose Alexander Karadjordjević as the new prince of Serbia. Officially, Turkey sought to bring peace between Mihailo and the Council, but in actuality she sided increasingly with the latter. Mihailo was driven from the throne by an armed revolt, which was the first example in modern Serbia of the use of the army for political purposes.[2]

Defenders of the Constitution and Their Program

The principal personalities in the Defenders of the Constitution regime were Vučić, Avram Petronijević, the brothers Simić (Aleksa and Stojan), Hadži-Milutin Garašanin and his son Ilija.[3] They took on the name Defenders of the Constitution during their struggle with Prince Mihailo. In order to justify and to popularize their opposition to him, they told the people that they were not rebelling against the prince, but only defending the constitution from him. Perhaps the most important and most colorful leader among them was Vučić. He had "all of the qualities necessary for a national-party leader: courage, decisiveness, mixing with people, influence on the masses, and great demagogic capability. He knew how to win a man and to strongly tie him to himself."[4] He knew how to represent everything that he wanted to do as the wish and need of the people. He told the people that they were all equal, that they did not need to stand up for anyone or to take off their hats in front of anyone. All of us, he said, have a right to hold our heads high, and none of us need stand in the shade, for all of us have a right to be warmed by the sun.[5]

By concentrating on the unpopular actions of Miloš and Mihailo, the Council won considerable popularity.[6] But the Council's most important leaders did not have political or reforming ideas, and neither did Prince Alexander. This was not true of the intellectuals who were in the civil service, mainly Serbs from Austria who had come to

Serbia after its liberation from the Turks. Vučić did not care for these Serbs but he did not have an alternative. Their main ideas were to establish personal security for the citizens, and to limit the prince.[7]

These ideas were to be implemented through the creation of courts, a bureaucracy, and institutions (written laws, schools, etc.) that would tie them together. This was the beginning of detailed administrative organization in Serbia. Personal rights, although not political, were secured. And the prince was limited by an oligarchical center, although not by the people. By comparison with the past, these were to be relative gains. The very existence of the collegial Council protected the people against personal absolutism. In brief, the first steps were being taken toward a rudimentary modernization of the Serbian nation.

Credit must be given to the Defenders of the Constitution in that they perceived, in somewhat primitive and difficult circumstances, the need for some form of modernization. They saw the need to organize the judiciary and the civil service, and to establish an educational system that would provide the personnel for both. In these undertakings, they achieved considerable success. In the realm of economic modernization, as we shall see, their vision and their actions left much to be desired.

First Steps Toward Modernization

One of the first steps taken by the new regime was the promulgation of a Civil Code in 1844, which in the main followed the Austrian example.[8] Moreover, many changes were made in court organization, introducing for the first time a hierarchy of courts. These changes were made over a period of years, but it is significant to note that before the end of the Council regime, the judicial power was separated from the prince.

Perhaps the most difficult problem was that of unqualified judges. At the time of the adoption of the Civil Code, only one of the presiding justices had a law degree. Three were illiterate, ten literate only to the extent that they could sign their names. And three had studied beyond elementary school.[9] Of the other judges: 21 were illiterate, 14 barely literate, 15 had more than an elementary education, and one was a law graduate. By 1853, the situation had improved, but not greatly. In that year, of 242 judges, 16 were illiterate, 76 had finished elementary school, 69 had a secondary (gymnasium) education, 13 had divinity training, 19 had studied philosophy, and 49 (or 20%) had law degrees.[10] By 1858, the number of really qualified judges numbered no more than one-fourth of the total.

The situation with lawyers was even worse. In fact, most of the law work was done by individual civil servants when their regular duties permitted. These were in the main court secretaries and clerks. This practice was forbidden in 1843, and subsequently a type of attorney did develop, mainly from among men who had failed at other things.[11] These men, through large fees and unsuccessful cases, brought about a distrust of lawyers among the populace which was to endure for a long time in Serbian public life. In turn, they attempted to put the blame on the courts.

Despite the efforts of the Council to create a suitable judiciary, there were constant complaints concerning the courts. The most frequently heard complaint was the slowness with which the courts acted. As the years went by the backlog of cases increased. This was due in part to poorly qualified judges, a condition which led to permission to appeal all cases. Some of the most affected persons, as a result of the slowness of the courts, were the importers who had to pay for goods on rigid schedules, but who had difficulty in collecting from merchants in the interior.

The Defenders of the Constitution wanted to have courts as good as any in the more modern nations, and this was popular with the people. The slowness of the courts, however, led people to see only the shortcomings. Moreover, they could not appreciate the growing formalism of the courts. According to Professor Jovanović, this assessment was unfair: "Even though full of shortcomings, the organization of the courts by the Defenders of the Constitution was of great historical significance. That was the first attempt to get modern European courts in place of the patriarchal ones."[12]

The problems of the civil service were similar to those of the judiciary. During Miloš's regime, civil servants were looked upon as his personal servants. They did not enjoy any greater standing than ordinary citizens. Their position was not determined by any law. There were no set tasks, no hierarchy, and no set pay.[13] Miloš's opponents wanted, first of all, to improve the status of the civil servants, because they knew from first hand experience what it was like to serve under him. With the Constitution of 1838 and subsequent legislation, civil servants became servants of the state, with detailed provisions as to their rights and privileges, even though these were not always lived up to in practice. Classes and pay scales were introduced, and bureaucrats could not be dismissed without cause. In addition, they got titles and uniforms, and they were required to be clean shaven. They were forbidden, however, from engaging in trade or other private pursuits.

Under these improved conditions, many men sought a career in the public service. The chief motive for going to school was the hope of landing a government job. But job security had some disadvantages. Because the top authorities did not have the right of disciplinary dismissal of bureaucrats without going to court, they resorted to transfers. Because of poor communication facilities, especially transport, transfers often resembled exile. On the other hand, the bureaucrats had great authority and no concern about public opinion, since criticism of the government was not permitted. One of the ministers even declared that "Government is the tutor, and the people are the pupils." By and large the people accepted the notion that they should obey the bureaucracy.

Nevertheless, there were complaints about the civil servants. As tutors, they were not much better educated than the pupils. Secondly, most of those who were educated had migrated from Austria, and were increasingly looked upon as foreigners. Moreover, the police became unpopular, in part because they had the right to impose sentences of 25 to 30 lashes or prison terms up to 30 days. Finally, the Defenders of the Constitution initially made many enemies through their dismissal of known or suspected Obrenović partisans in the civil service.[14] In addition, toward the end of the Council regime, the bureaucrats were brought into the conflict that had developed between the prince and the Council, because both sides in the conflict sought allies among them.

While it is not easy to pass judgment, it seems clear that the Constitutional Defenders did create a legally secure position for the bureaucracy. While bringing about some improvements in the quality of the civil service, they did not greatly develop its professional competence. Moreover, the conflicts at the top, those between the prince and the Council, as well as those within the Council, prevented the attainment of a firm and disciplined control over the bureaucracy.

The emphasis that the Defenders of the Constitution placed on education and the judiciary is indicated by the fact that only in these domestic areas did they establish separate ministries, with practically everything else being under the ministry of the interior. Their main aim was to create a bureaucratic intelligentsia with which to staff the civil service and the courts. To this end they increased the number of schools, and they created agricultural trade, and military academies. The number of schools increased from 72 (with 2,514 students) in 1835-36 to 343 (with 10,518 students) in 1857-58.[15] Even so, about two-thirds of Serbia's communities were without schools. The first law courses were inaugurated in 1841, and the National Library was established in 1853.

Initially, the local communities *(opštine)* built schools and paid the teachers, with the central authority merely exercising a supervisory function. In the 1850s, however, the teachers were selected and paid by the ministry of education. This was made possible in part by the enactment of a special school tax in 1855, the proceeds of which went into a special school fund instead of the state treasury.[16] Generally, however, conditions for teachers were not good. Pay was low and irregular, and teachers were not held in high esteem by the people.

In 1839, for the first time, Serbian students in modest numbers were sent to study abroad, some to Austria and Germany, but increasingly to France. By 1858, some 200 men had been educated abroad. Although a modest number, these men were to constitute the beginning of a native intelligentsia. They brought new ideas and elements of European culture. In general, they tended to be more European in outlook than the Serbs who had come from Austria, whose outlook was more provincial.

The first sign of dissatisfaction with the Constitutional Defenders' regime appeared among educated men, among students and professors.[17] There were instances where the minister had or had not finished elementary school, whereas his secretary had a Paris doctorate. These younger men began to speak openly and critically. They did not agree with the Council that authority should be respected just because it was authority. They recognized the need of an institution that would represent and defend the people's rights. Parliament was such an institution, but the Serbian *Skupština* did not exist during the Council regime. It met only once (1848) in a period of twenty years.

At the time that the Council oligarchy came to power, Serbia was economically backward in every way. Agricultural techniques were medieval. There were few roads, little money, and no economic organization on a national scale. There were scarcely any engineers or other technical personnel. Unfortunately, the oligarchy did very little about Serbia's economic backwardness.

A postal service was organized in 1843, and the first telegraph was installed in 1855. Some efforts were made to promote capital formation, including the creation of a national bank. But financial loans continued to be difficult to get, and the interest rates remained high. Gains in agriculture, mining, and forestry were minimal or worse. Adjustments to a money economy were not made.

Professor Jovanović has said that in administratively despotic countries, more than anywhere else, the government is duty bound to improve the material welfare of the people—this is its only justification.[18] Without minimizing the achievements of the oligarchy in the fields of education, judiciary, and the civil service, it still must be said that the Constitutional Defenders were less than adequate in constructing roads, promoting trade, providing financing for economic development, and in protecting the forests from indiscriminate cutting. Their failures were not necessarily due to lack of concern. Technically, they were unprepared, and financially they were committed to low taxes and therefore did not have the money. These failures tended to make the people forget what the Council had done in the bureaucratic, judicial, and educational fields.

Interestingly enough, there were few, if any, organized and politically active interest groups at this time. Agitation for social and economic change, to the extent that it existed, was being undertaken by the political elite, and not the other way around. This western educated elite welcomed Serbia's economic orientation toward Western Europe following the Paris Peace Conference (1856), at which the Great Powers assumed the role of Serbia's protector, a role which Russia had played until that time although in a somewhat ill-defined manner.

In the field of public finance, the country was faced with chronic deficits.[19] This was contrary to Miloš's time when the national treasury had surpluses. The Council regime's initial popularity was in part the result of its promise of low taxes. On the other hand, its creation of new institutions and the incurring of additional costs, as in the case of the military, required additional money. The government was afraid to raise taxes and instead turned to palliatives. The result was greater deficits. Only with the Budget Law of 1858 was there a serious effort to bring some sort of order in public finance.

By far the most important tax was a type of head tax. The local communities paid five *talirs* per person, but they were instructed, in collecting the tax, to pay attention to the relative wealth of individuals. Local communities tended to ignore this, with the result that the poorer citizens were the hardest hit. Late in its rule, the regime did raise taxes on exports, court costs, and forest cutting but the income from these was not significant. The government was in such difficult financial straits that had it continued to rule after 1858, it would have been forced to raise taxes considerably.

Developing Crisis in the Regime

In theory, under the Constitution of 1838, supreme authority was shared by the prince and the Council. Although its provisions were not always precise, and in some respects contradictory, no real difficulties arose until the prince and the Council came into conflict.[20] The Council, consisting of 17 members, was to be chosen by the prince from among the best known and most respected men among the people. But the law on the organization of the Council (1839), made it impossible for the prince to choose anyone who was not recommended by the Council. Once appointed, members of the Council could not be removed.[21] The Council began as a group of eminent and popular leaders from their respective districts, for the most part men of relative wealth, but in twenty years the members of this self-perpetuating oligarchy were little known outside the capital.

The Constitution vested legislative initiative in the Council. The prince could only recommend that the Council appoint a commission to look into the need for legislation on a certain subject. He had no decree power, but he could veto Council proposals. Moreover, the Council had control over the budget. In addition, the Council determined the administrative organization of the government and had the power to oversee the work of ministers. And the prince was required to appoint his ministers from among Council members. In this way, the ministers became, in effect, a committee of the Council.

The basic conflict between the prince and the Council, as it emerged, concerned control of the administration. This was first made evident in the military field, because the prince wanted the army personally loyal to him.[22] The prince also held that he was the chief of government, and needed to seek agreement with the Council only in the area of legislation. By the mid-1850s, the prince asserted the right not only to appoint ministers from men outside the Council, but also to appoint Council members without the Council's prior recommendation.[23] The Council resented the action of the prince but could do little. At different times in their quarrels, the Council and the prince sought the help of the Porte, but the latter was inclined to let Serbian matters disentangle themselves.

The conflict between the Council and the prince was exacerbated by virtue of the fact that the prince was appointing his wife's close relatives to high posts.[24] Important men, among them friends of his, told Alexander that he was pursuing an unwise course, but he apparently was unable to resist the demands of his wife's family.[25]

The conflict had entered its third year, when in September 1857 the government uncovered a plot to kill the prince.[26] The President of the Council, Stefan Stefanović Tenka, and the President of the Supreme Court, Cvetko Rajović, as well as other members of the Council were involved. It became known as Tenka's conspiracy *(Tenkina zavera)*. The aims and motives were not very clear, although some of the conspirators seemed to have feared that the prince might strike first.[27] The conspirators were found guilty and sentenced to death, but because of the Porte's intervention, Alexander was afraid to sign the death warrant. Rather, he commuted the sentences to life-imprisonment in chains.

Several other Council members were threatened with arrest unless they resigned. Six did so immediately, and their applications for pensions were approved. This was before the conspirators had been tried and sentenced. Four other Council members were subsequently forced out. As might have been expected, the new Council was made up of men loyal to Alexander, some of them his own relatives.

Before long, however, a "loyal opposition" developed in the Council, not so much against the prince as against his ministers. But the more important opposition developed outside the Council. It consisted of the former Council members, who argued that their being forced out was in fact a coup on the part of the prince, and therefore contrary to the Constitution of 1838. Thereupon they appealed to the Porte and to the Great Powers who were the guarantors of Serbia's independence. The Porte wanted to promote peace between the Council and the prince, because she did not want the European powers to intervene. Russia and France asserted that Alexander had carried out a coup. All three did not like Alexander's pro-Austrianism, and succeeded in forcing him to accept a compromise.

The "compromise" with the old Council was actually a defeat for Alexander. Under its terms the prince forgave the Council for its opposition, and the Council forgave the prince for illegalities. The six members initially forced out were returned to the Council. A new law on the organization of the Council was promised, which would resolve all disputed questions. All of this really favored the Council. Alexander accepted the degrading "compromise" because he had lived in such fear of being deposed that this looked like a relative gain. In the process he lost whatever prestige he had enjoyed with the public. He seemed weak—he could not even keep in prison the men who had conspired to kill him. The Council, on the other hand, appeared strong.

The new law on the organization of the Council further weakened the prince.[28] His one-time absolute veto became merely suspensive. The criminal responsibility of Council members was so hemmed in that prior approval of the Council was required before a Council member could be brought to court. The principle that ministers would be selected only from men that the Council proposed was strengthened anew. Moreover, the Council gained additional powers of control over ministers, including the power to reprimand them and thus possibly to force them to resign. This was a rudimentary attempt to establish political responsibility in Serbia. It should also be mentioned that the new law made it impossible even for distant relatives of the prince to serve as Council members. The new organization of the Council represented the pinnacle of Council power. It was the master of legislative as well as administrative power.

One man who was to play a critical role in the struggle between the prince and the Council was Ilija Garašanin.[29] The son of a well-to-do merchant, he had had a private teacher, but he had also travelled extensively in Europe. Originally a member of the Council oligarchy, he developed into a good practical administrator. He served some ten years (1843-1852) as minister of interior, a longer uninterrupted service in that post than any other man in previous Serbian history. Because of his known anti-Russian attitude, he was forced out of Serbian politics as a result of Russian pressure.

Because of his ability and loyalty to the prince, however, Garašanin was soon brought back as minister of foreign affairs. One of his first acts was to dismiss Vučić as cabinet advisor.[30] But Alexander and Garašanin soon came into conflict simply because the prince did not wish to listen to advice from his ministers. He wanted them merely to carry out his orders. Following a temporary peace between the two, Alexander again bowed to Russian pressure and dismissed Garašanin.[31] Because he did not wish to return to the Council, Garašanin was given a pension. After the Peace of Paris in 1856, however, he was returned to the Council and again made minister of interior. In that post he was soon to play a key role in the downfall of the prince and the Council.

It should be pointed out, parenthetically, that Garašanin was a far-sighted leader, whose services to the nation did not end with the overthrow of the oligarchy in 1858. He was a systematic man; he had a foreign and domestic policy program for Serbia. In foreign affairs his basic position was that Serbia should not ally herself with either Russia or Austria, but should turn toward the western powers, first of all France.[32] Of the older group of leaders, Garašanin seemed to be the only one in whom the rising new generation of liberal leaders, often referred to as *Parislije* because of their Paris education, had some trust. Some referred to him as the link between the oldsters and the *Parislije*.

In the final analysis, the conflict between the prince and the Council meant that the nation had two masters neither of which would let the other one govern. Just as at one time a need was felt to divide too concentrated authority, in the late 1850s a need was felt for some concentration of a too divided authority. As this need became greater, the fall of Alexander and the Constitutional Defenders became all the more inescapable.

Revolution of 1858

In 1858, the regime of the Defenders of the Constitution was overthrown by the Skupština. Both the prince and the Council were removed in the most peaceful revolution in Serbian history. It was called St. Andrew's *(Svetoandrejska)* Skupština because it was scheduled to meet on St. Andrew's day. What follows is but the briefest of accounts of how that Skupština was called, what it did, and how it did it.[33]

Two important leaders, Vučić and Garašanin, decided after the failure to the conspiracy to kill Alexander that he must nevertheless somehow be removed. Efforts to oust him with the aid of the Porte and/or certain European powers had failed. And the conspiracy to kill him had misfired. The only way left was to have the Skupština overthrow him. But calling the Skupština was not easy. There were no established means for doing so, and the prince was not in favor of calling it. Moreover, some of the members of the Council were not for convoking it because they feared that the Skupština would simply become the tool of the master demagogue Vučić.

Vučić traveled around agitating among the people for the calling of the Skupština. He had one demagogic speech in which he criticized the bureaucracy and called for reduced taxes, asserting that only the Skupština could save the "wretched people." Garašanin operated more cautiously, working through Obrenović followers and the young liberal intellectuals. The former had been badly persecuted but gained considerable courage as Alexander's reputation and prestige fell. The liberal intellectuals, imbued with the spirit of the nation's heroic past, did not particularly respect either the prince or the Council. Moreover, the idea of the Skupština appealed to them because it was similar to parliaments in western Europe, with which they had become familiar.

When the terrain had been prepared, Garašanin, without consulting the prince in advance, raised in the Council the question of calling the Skupština, asserting that in no other way could order be secured in the nation. He met with some opposition in the Council, but subsequently got its approval and that of the prince. The latter was reluctant but he did not know what to do if Garašanin should resign. Moreover, he thought that loyal persons could be selected as members of the Skupština.

Under the law for the calling of the Skupština, there were two types of representatives: (1) those chosen by the people, and (2) those who were entitled to seats by virtue of their positions. In the latter category were representatives of the judiciary, administration, and the church, for a total of 63 deputies. Of the 376 deputies chosen by the people, those in the cities were elected directly and those in the countryside indirectly. Because neither Alexander's partisans nor Garašanin wanted Vučić in the Skupština, the law provided that Council members and certain other officials would not be eligible for election. In addition, the law specified that the president and the vice-president of the Skupština must be chosen from among its members.

Once the deputies had been chosen, it was fairly obvious that most of the members of the Skupština, many of them Obrenović followers, were hostile to Alexander. The prince and his group still had that solace which has been the undoing of so many regimes: "They will not dare!" More than that, they did not think that Vučić and Garašanin would join the Obrenović crowd. Finally, the prince was confident that as a last resort the army would defend him.[34]

There were three primary centers of opposition to Alexander: (1) the Vučić-Garašanin group, (2) the united liberal-Obrenović group, and (3) Miloš Obrenović's personal agents. The whole atmosphere in Belgrade, with many of the deputies coming on horseback and armed, seemed anti-Alexander. But there was no agreement among the opponents as to who or what should be put in his place. Certainly, Vučić and Garašanin did not want Miloš's return. Garašanin's opponents even spread rumors that he wanted to be prince of Serbia, and many people believed them.[35] The liberals, for their part, were willing to support the return of the Obrenović dynasty provided they could secure the establishment of a powerful parliament.

Certain liberal leaders became the main tacticians in the situation. Their plan may be summarized under four points: (1) the initiative for the overthrow of Alexander would be left to Garašanin and his well-to-do cohorts; (2) before deposing the prince, the liberals would propose a new law which would endow the Skupština with considerable power and which would guarantee its meeting annually, thus assuring support for the proposal on the part of those who were not really for it but who still needed the Skupština's support to overthrow the prince; (3) as soon as the prince would be overthrown, the liberals would propose that the powers of the prince would be entrusted temporarily to the Skupština, thus avoiding a Vučić-Garašanin regency; and (4) at the moment that Alexander would be overthrown, the Skupština would proclaim Miloš Obrenović prince.[36] The principal liberal tactician was Jevrem Grujić, who was chosen as one of the two secretaries of the Skupština.[37]

Grujić's role was enhanced by virtue of the fact that the liberals' proposal for a new law concerning the Skupština became the first order of business. Moreover, during the discussion of this project, which took several days, he was its presiding officer. The man who had been elected the Skupština's president, Miša Anastasijević, did not attend the sessions until the day that the proposal to oust Alexander was to be raised.

The liberals' project for future Skupštinas was far too radical a document for many of the influential delegates. Garašanin and his crowd, for example, were opposed to it, but went along with it after the liberals agreed that once passed, the project should be submitted to the Council for approval. The law was passed on these terms, but the attitude of the Skupština, which was convoked to depose the prince, is depicted by Jovanović as follows: "If I can overthrow the prince, then I can do everything else; there are no more limits to my power."[38]

Having succeeded in getting the law on the Skupština passed, the liberals left the initiative for the overthrow of Alexander in the hands of others.[39] This was not slow in coming, with the Skupština quickly reaching a verdict that it should ask for the prince's resignation. Its wishes were put forth in a written document, which also enunciated the principle that Serbia was an elective monarchy. A delegation was sent to deliver the document to the prince, while at the same time taking along a resignation for him to sign. He did not oblige, but asked for 24 hours to think it over. He thereupon called a meeting of the Council, most of whose members advised him to resign. Since he did not wish to do so, he fled to the fortress, i.e., to the headquarters of the Turkish *paša* for protection.[40]

By this act, the prince left the command of the armed forces in the hands of the minister of interior, Garašanin, who wanted the Council and the Skupština to agree on a provisional government. But the liberals and the Obrenović followers were impatient in this period of uncertainty, particularly in view of what the army might do. Without delay, they succeeded in having the Skupština declare Alexander ousted, elect Miloš as the new prince, declare that the regency power would be in the hands of the Skupština, and made Stevča Mihailović commandant of the armed forces and the police. All of this was proclaimed to the public outside even before the various acts had been properly signed.

The groundwork for these acts had been prepared the night before when it was learned that Alexander had fled to the city fortress, seeking Turkish protection. Moreover, armed mobs, made up mostly of Obrenović supporters, were mobilized so as to provide a kind of shield around the brewery building in which the Skupština was meeting. The barracks of the Belgrade garrison were menacingly close— right across the street!

The Skupština merely informed the Council of its actions. It did not seek its approval. Vučić, although not a member, was permitted to speak to the Skupština. He sought to nullify the choice of Miloš, pointing out that the Council's assent was necessary. But Vučić could no longer sway mass gatherings as he once did. But getting Garašanin to give up control of the armed forces was another matter. He did not waver even when the mobs were in front of his house demanding that he abide by the Skupština's wishes.

There is agreement among Serbian scholars that the army could have resolved the matter in Alexander's favor. It did not do so because there was a realization on the part of key men that in the process bloodshed could not be avoided, and they were unwilling to have that happen. Moreover, while realizing that he had lost control of events, Garašanin was for peace and order. He had his trusted men in the barracks who would act only on his orders.

In the end Garašanin agreed to surrender control of the armed forces when liberal leaders assented to the formation of a provisional government, consisting of Garašanin, Stevča Mihailović, and one other person. Just as he had asked of the army to remain at peace, he asked of the Skupština to stay within boundaries of the law. More than anyone else, he deserves the credit for the avoidance of a real military clash between the army and the Skupština.

With the fall of Alexander, the regime of the Defenders of the Constitution also came to an end. A revolution which they had prepared turned out to be as much a revolution against them as against the prince. Originally popular, the oligarchy, over the years, lost contact with the people. In the end they, too, were held responsible for the state of the nation. And the people's representatives, in an emotionally charged atmosphere, once again turned to the Obrenović dynasty.

ENLIGHTENED DESPOTISM, 1859-1868

The overthrow of the Council oligarchy and of Alexander in 1858, and the return of the Obrenović dynasty, ushered in a period of nearly ten years of absolute monarchical rule. Prince Miloš, who had been forced to abdicate in 1838, came back to rule for less than two years, passing away in 1860 at the age of 80. His son, Mihailo, who had been forced to flee Serbia in 1842, succeeded him. Mihailo's reign of some eight years has most often been described as enlightened despotism. It was a period in which absolute monarchical rule was little challenged, and generally accepted.[1]

Miloš's Reign, 1859-1860

Upon his return to Serbia in January 1859, Miloš talked of governing as a constitutional monarch. During his first reign men lost their heads because of that word constitution. But Miloš had not really changed; he came back with the same concept of governing authority with which he left in 1839. In his view, the constitution of 1838, which had limited his powers, had ceased to exist at the moment that the Skupština had called him back. He openly told the Turkish representative in Belgrade that he would not respect that constitution.

Although the Skupština had returned him to the throne in December 1858, Miloš waited in Bucharest until the Porte had acted favorably on the question of his return. In the interim, his supporters in the Skupština were doing some of his work for him. An act of the Skupština declared a lack of confidence in the Council members and ministers, on the basis of which Miloš could subsequently dismiss them. Similarly, the Skupština had also declared itself in favor of a thorough cleaning out of the civil servants. In making his far-reaching personnel changes, therefore, Miloš could assert that he was only carrying out the people's wishes.

Miloš really wanted to abolish the Council, but when he concluded that this was impossible, he sought to make it innocuous. In the main he selected national elders from his first reign, ordinary and uneducated men. Moreover, he changed their oath so that in the future they would be loyal to him and not, as theretofore, also to the Turkish Sultan. In addition, because the prestige of the Skupština had risen as that of the Council had declined, the Council caused no real difficulties to either Miloš or to Mihailo.

Miloš had no problem with his ministers either. They served at his pleasure, and he changed them frequently. He expected them to carry out his orders without raising any questions. Some things (e.g., the army and the Belgrade police) he kept under his personal control and did not even tell his ministers what he was doing.[2] Jevrem Grucjić, who was in effect president of the council of ministers, began to act as the head of a parliamentary government, giving Miloš advice and setting forth requests. But Miloš did not understand this new era. Grujić sought to explain ministerial responsibility to him, but this did not appeal to Miloš. "What am I," he asked Grujić, "If you take responsibility for me?" In such circumstances, Grujić could not remain a minister for long.

The epuration of the civil service, however, presented greater difficulties.[3] One of the real contributions of the Constitutional Defenders regime had been the organization of a more competent bureaucracy, whose members could be removed only through court action. The liberals, who had been influential in the overthrow of the Council and the return of Miloš, wanted a cleansing of the civil service. Miloš went along with them, because he could not conceive of a bureaucracy having any independence or rights. But the epuration of the bureaucracy created problems: some able civil servants were dismissed as a result of personal vendettas, and in some localities men were being chosen in local taverns. The latter especially was not to Miloš' taste since he viewed it as an encroachment on his authority. Subsequently, he was to blame the liberals for excesses in the epuration process.[4]

Miloš knew that the Council regime had become unpopular in part because of the unresponsiveness of the bureaucracy. Hence, he was sure that some of his actions against the bureaucracy would meet with popular acclaim. For example, a whole gradation of titles had been established for civil servants, which Miloš abolished. Thereafter all of them were to have the simple title of mister. But Miloš went further. All rights of the bureaucracy, which had been secured by the Constitution of 1838, were trampled upon. "Neither the civil servants' tenure and rank, nor their rights to pay and pensions were respected."[5]

Miloš was less successful in his efforts to interfere with the judicial process. The courts had established such independence that Miloš could not force them to rule contrary to the law. He could only take satisfaction in cursing out judges whose rulings he did not like, and he accorded himself that satisfaction in full measure.

The Skupština, of all governmental institutions under Miloš, was in some ways the most significant, not because it was strong enough to limit him—a power it did not have—but because he allowed it to have full freedom of speech. This was his way of being informed about the people's complaints and needs. Here the people spoke; in all other political institutions only Miloš spoke.

Miloš appears to have had two basic policy aims: (1) to secure his governing power, and (2) to please the peasant masses. Although the Porte would not recognize anew the hereditary rights of the Obrenović dynasty, she did not object to recognizing Mihailo, who had no children, as Miloš's heir. Although he could not get rid of his opponents as he once could, Miloš was nevertheless able, through arrests, pressures, etc., to isolate or neutralize them so that they constituted no danger to the regime.[6]

In order to bring some satisfaction to the peasant masses, Miloš issued a number of decrees that were designed to speed up judicial processes. Ironically, in the beginning this helped the money lenders most in collecting debts from the peasants. One of the crucial problems of the peasant was the high interest rates. Miloš wanted to come to the aid of the peasant, proclaiming the principle that the land belongs to him who works it. The liberals argued that the answer was to be found in government loans at low interest rates. The conservatives, on the other hand, told him that the peasants' troubles stemmed from their lack of knowledge as to how to work the land, and from the fact that there were too many holidays and too much time spent in taverns. Therefore cheap credit would solve nothing.

Neither the conservatives nor the liberals gave Miloš what he wanted—a quick solution. He took some suggestions from both groups. In addition, he decreed that with respect to past debts the peasant would have to pay only what he swore (in church) that he owed.[7] Although popular, this measure created much confusion, particularly because false oaths were not a rarity. One of the consequences was that creditors stopped making loans. It is of interest that this decree was abolished when Mihailo came to the throne.

The peasants also complained about taxes on forest cutting. Miloš abolished them. They also complained about contributing to the local food depositories, which were designed to have sufficient food reserves for three years in case of bad crop years. The contributions were due to be increased so as to provide a reserve for six years. Miloš rescinded the projected increases.

In brief, Miloš followed a policy of concessions, of letting up, of opportunism. For a time he permitted the conservative forces to speak out in the official or semi-official press. Then he changed editors and permitted the liberals to answer back.[8] Initially popular, Miloš's regime soon became unbearable for conservatives and liberals alike. It was a despotism that was fickle and equivocating. The one-time legendary hero, as death neared, changed from day to day and seemingly without a steady course or definite direction.[9]

Mihailo's Reign, 1860-1869

Mihailo came to power with one major aim—war against the Turks.[10] More ambitious than his father, he wanted to stir up all Balkan peoples to revolt, with Serbia leading the way and ultimately playing the major role in the creation of a South Slav state. To this end, it was necessary to prepare for war. To accomplish this and to unite all Serbs in a patriotic zeal required, in Mihailo's view, the elimination of party squabbles and the concentration of all authority in the hands of the ruler.

In domestic affairs, Mihailo wanted to strengthen legality and to improve the material welfare of the country. He believed that legality could be established only by a ruler who was above parties. Similarly, only such a ruler could raise the material welfare of the people. Mihailo was surprised by the backwardness of Serbia's agriculture, the low cultural level of the people, the poverty, and the primitive nature of life. People in such a condition, in his opinion, could be extricated from misery only by an enlightened despot.[11]

Understandably, he could not say anything openly about war with Turkey, but he did indicate the need of a national army which would provide security and defense. His other aims were stated openly, in a proclamation when he came to power in 1860 and in his speech from the throne to the Skupština in 1861. With respect to legality, he said: "As long as Prince Mihailo is on the throne, every one should know that law is the highest will in Serbia, to which every one without distinction must submit."[12]

Mihailo's Political Institutions

In order to realize his program, Mihailo believed that he had to make peace among the domestic factions, and to change the constitution. He could not hope to seek his patriotic aims unless the warring parties or factions could be brought together. And he did not believe that he could strengthen his authority while saddled with the

Constitution of 1838, whose aim was to weaken the monarch.

Characteristic of Mihailo's attitude toward government in Serbia was his assertion that he could count on his fingers all men in Serbia "who have a European education. There are no more than ten or twelve of them. The institutions of a country are not created for the twelve most educated men in it. . . . To grant parliamentarianism only because then Milovan Janković and a few others could give parliamentary speeches would be frivolous."[13] He felt that the people were not ripe for a representative system. In commenting upon an address given to him by the Skupština, he said to one of its secretaries: "Did you see how many crosses there were on the address which you gave me? As long as members of the Skupština cannot even sign their names . . . your haste to proclaim great freedoms is in vain."[14] Moreover, Mihailo saw in the Serbian masses people with anarchistic tendencies. How can you view the people as the source of all authority, he asked rhetorically, when they seek to negate all authority.[15]

When Mihailo came to power there were discussions concerning a new constitution. While modified to a degree by the law of 1858 concerning the Skupština, the Constitution of 1838 was theoretically still in force, and presumably its amendment would require Turkish approval. By 1860, however, Turkish power for all practical purposes was non-existent in Serbia, although it was not until 1867 that Serbia saw the last of the Turks. The Great Powers nevertheless advised Mihailo not to adopt a new constitution which might cause a conflict with the Porte. On the other hand, Serbian leaders were advised to promulgate certain laws of a constitutional nature. Several organic laws, dealing with the Council, the Skupština, and the central administration were soon adopted. This collection of laws constituted Mihailo's political and administrative system.

The law concerning the Council (1861) transformed this once all-powerful body into an ordinary bureaucratic instrument of the prince. The prince appointed its members in the same way that he appointed civil servants, and he had in a certain measure disciplinary powers over them. Council members did not enjoy any special privileges. Only once during Mihailo's reign was a question of principled difference raised by one of the Council's memebers. This question concerned the responsibility of ministers (to the Council), but the Council was told in no uncertain terms by the premier (Ilija Garašanin) that all opposition would be viewed as directed against the prince and against the state. As time went along, the Council's functions became more and more legal-administrative.

The laws concerning the organization of governmental authority gave the prince unlimited power over his ministers and over the bureaucracy.[17] One law established a council of ministers, with a president. The ministries were: foreign affairs, interior, justice, education and religion, finance, war, and public works. The ministers were made responsible to the prince. Another law took away the tenure of civil servants, enabling the regime to appoint and dismiss at will.

Late in Mihailo's regime another law tightened controls over local government (*opština* or commune). While some writers have viewed this as a blow to local government, Slobodan Jovanović asserts that not much local government existed in any case. The main functions of the *opština*, he says, were judicial and police, and hence mainly administrative.[18] Moreover, he says, the *opština* did not have the economic requisites for self-government. Finally, the local community prided itself on the election of the local chief, the *kmet*, but once elected he could be removed only by state authority and not by the people.

The law on the Skupština disappointed those who in 1858 had sought to give it such great importance.[19] Gone were the paragraphs about the sovereignty of the Skupština, ministerial responsibility, and freedom of the press. Disappointing also was the proviso that the Skupština would meet every three years instead of annually. Similarly, the Skupština now had merely consultative power, when the ministers sought its advice, which was rarely. It could not amend bills, and it could not make legislative proposals of its own. Moreover, the elections of its members were openly and significantly influenced by the police. In the light of these considerations, the law on the Skupština was a backward step in its evolution, but its long term effect was to add to its institutionalization.

By and large, the regime did not experience any serious difficulties with the three Skupštinas that were held during Mihailo's reign. During the last one, however, about one-fourth of the deputies demanded that the Skupština be given legislative powers, that ministerial responsibility be instituted, and that a law on the freedom of the press be adopted.[20] These demands were largely cries in the wilderness.

Mihailo recognized the importance of the press, mainly as a way of educating the public. But aside from the semi-official press, he did not permit any other. Private efforts to establish a political newspaper were impeded at every turn. The only exception was *Srbija*, which was granted permission to publish in 1867, with the provision that it

stay away from domestic politics, a prohibition it managed to cir-
cumvent from time to time. Opponents of Mihailo's regime, however, were editing critical newspapers abroad, in Geneva *(Sloboda)*,
in Novi Sad *(Dnevnik)*, and in Budapest *(Zastava)*. The former two
were founded in 1864 and the latter one in 1866. Their importation
into Serbia was forbidden, but a sufficient number of copies came
through so that at least all educated men in Belgrade knew what
they were writing.

Mihailo's Regime in Action

Mihailo was aware that the dynastic question was the principal
cause of domestic discord, and he sought to end it.[21] In his efforts
to promote domestic peace, he was forgiving and he sought forgive-
ness. He permitted Karadjordjević partisans, who had fled or were
forced to leave Serbia, to return. Those who had unlawfully lost
their pensions had them reinstated or they were returned to government service. And he attempted to justify injustices done to civil
servants.

For his ministers, Mihailo wanted to select leading men from the
liberal and conservative groups. The conservative leaders, Ilija
Garašanin and Jovan Marinović, did not wish to sully themselves by
associating with the liberals, Stevča Mihailović and Jevrem Grujić.
Thereupon Mihailo appointed a neutral ministry headed by Filip
Hristić. Before a year was out, however, it became evident that Mihailo
could not govern with a ministry of bureaucrats who had little political strength.

Since uniting of the factions was impossible, Mihailo turned to
the conservatives in 1861, appointing a ministry headed by Garašanin,
a ministry that stayed in power until 1867. Mihailo had expected to
keep the conservative group on a leash, because he did not want any
persecution of the liberals. He soon gave in, and in a matter of two
or three years all the more important liberals were driven out of government service. In Jovanović's words, "Mihailo's whole regime was
one long struggle between conservatives and liberals."[22]

In the judicial realm, Mihailo began his regime with emphasis on
the rule of law, yet in 1864 he found himself jailing five judges of
the Supreme Court, presumably the highest guarantor of legality.[23]
They were found guilty, by a specially constituted court, of intentionally distorting the law and wrongly judging. They were sentenced
to three years of imprisonment, but were pardoned after they had
served something over a year of their sentences.

In the winter of 1863 the police had allegedly uncovered a conspiracy to overthrow the dynasty, and some thirty to forty persons were arrested. There had been meetings and talk, but there was some question as to whether any preparations had been undertaken in order to carry out the overthrow. The court having original jurisdiction dismissed charges against eight of the accused, but sentenced a number of men to prison terms of up to two years. When the matter came to the Supreme Court every one was set free, on the ground that all that had existed were confidential political discussions but there was no proof of attempted preparations for action.[24]

This ruling so alarmed the regime that it determined to take immediate action. In the normal course of events, the five judges should have been tried for any alleged misdeeds by the other members of the Supreme Court. Instead, the regime set up a special court, consisting of four members of the Council of State and three members of the Supreme Court, thus a majority of non-judges. This court based its decision of guilt on the findings of a three-man commission, and did not hear any of the accused judges.

The wrecking of the Supreme Court hurt Mihailo and his government. Until this event, the public in the main was inclined to believe that the liberals exaggerated in their criticism. But the ironic conclusion of this case, wherein the alleged conspirators went free while their judges went to jail, characterized Mihailo's regime as indisputably despotic, a characterization that remained until the end.

Mihailo's greatest achievement, in the opinion of most scholars, was his creation of a national army. The existence of the national army made a great impression on the people. National morale was high among peasants and intellectuals alike. Moreover, the considerable prestige which Serbia built up among the foreign powers was due in large measure to her military efforts. Mainly because of the army, Mihailo was successful in 1867 in forcing the Turks to remove their garrisons from Serbian cities—and without bloodshed.

But many people in Serbia were impatient for war with Turkey as a way of uniting Serbian lands which were still under Turkish rule. Mihailo spent a great deal of time in making alliances with other Balkan peoples, in the expectation that all of them would one day join in a common cause. Mihailo's chief helper was his premier and foreign minister, Garašanin. He was the first Serbian politician who realistically comprehended Serbia's diplomatic problems. In brief, he was distrustful of Russia and Austria, because help from either might easily lead to infringement of Serbian sovereignty. Therefore, Serbia must look west, mainly to France.

Because of Mihailo's marital difficulties, Garašanin left the cabinet in 1867. For some time people had been asking why war with Turkey was being postponed. Mihailo's new advisors created additional doubts. Moreover, French support for the Serbian cause weakened because of France's concern with Prussia. France needed Austrian support and was not therefore inclined to alienate her by actively helping Serbia.

The liberals now began to question Mihailo's sincerity with respect to liberating subjugated Serbs. Understandably, they acted almost solely in Serbian circles abroad. They attacked Mihailo on two counts: (1) they questioned whether he would act against the Turks, believing that he preferred postponement, and (2) they argued that to appeal to Serbs abroad, Mihailo's regime would have to be liberalized and democratized.[25] They insisted that the latter step was imperative if the war with Turkey was being postponed for whatever reason. While this criticism may not have penetrated deeply into Serbia, it served to create profound doubts among intellectuals with respect to Mihailo's foreign policy.

On the economic front, Mihailo's regime experienced meager gains. In ten years (1858-1868) government expenditures more than doubled (61%), but in its final years Mihailo's regime had a balanced budget. Having inherited chronic deficits, Mihailo had ideas about basic reforms in the tax structure. He sought to impose a property tax, but this met with such opposition among the peasants that it was soon dropped in favor of increasing already existing levies. In his effort to help the debt-ridden peasant, Mihailo created a special Fund Administration which provided loans at six per cent interest. In the end, this did not prove as helpful to the poor peasant as Mihailo had hoped. It should be added that Mihailo contributed large sums from his personal fortune, in loans and grants, to meet certain government expenditures.

Several great economic reforms were projected, but little came of them.[26] Plans with respect to railroads, river navigation, and the national bank never got beyond the investigation and planning stage. Some successes were achieved in mining and in the development of silk worms. The failure of the regime to do very much in the area of economic development was made worse by the fact that there were several bad agricultural years during Mihailo's reign. Some defenders of the regime placed great emphasis on the need to liberate subjugated Serbs first, leaving economic problems for a later day.

Mihailo's Marital Problems and Rift in Government

Mihailo's marital difficulties in the last three years of his reign led to acute differences among his ministers. His wife, Julia, was of Hungarian ancestry and a Roman Catholic. She was not popular in Belgrade, where her going to the Catholic church, especially when escorted by Mihailo, was regarded by the plain people as shameful. The fact that she did not have children was thought to be most unfortunate. The liberals regarded the marriage as a political mistake.

In early 1862, a love letter which Julia had written to Karl Arenburg came into Mihailo's hands.[27] Among other things, the letter spoke of her separation from Mihailo and of her life with Arenburg in Venice. Mihailo decided that the marriage must end, but the Turkish bombardment of Belgrade that summer seemed to bring them together again. Early in 1863, Mihailo sent her on a political mission to London. While abroad she got together with Arenburg, and wrote to Mihailo suggesting divorce. But he did not agree. In November 1864, she came back to Belgrade after an absence of nearly two years. In June 1865, Mihailo suggested divorce, but this time she refused. Finally, she left Serbia and did not return during his lifetime.

Toward the end of 1865, Mihailo and Julia reached an agreement to end the marriage in such a way that no mention would be made of the love letter to Arenburg. Moreover, Julia obtained a generous property settlement. As a Catholic, she could not get a divorce, but this might not have caused any serious problem had it not been for Mihailo's desire to marry again. Even this might have been tolerated except for the fact that the girl Mihailo wanted to marry, Katarina Konstantinović, was his second cousin. In 1865 he was a man of 40 and she a young girl of only sixteen.

The result was a serious rift among Mihailo's ministers. In the patriarchal Serbia of that day his divorce was looked upon as a scandal. His proposed marriage to his second cousin was regarded as worse than a scandal; it was incest and forbidden by the canons of the Serbian Orthodox faith. His ministers were willing to treat the divorce as his personal affair, but not the proposed marriage. The principal spokesman was the premier, Garašanin, and when he could not persuade the prince, he had to go. Mihailo dismissed him in 1867.

Some ministers were willing to accommodate Mihailo. He had consulted with a close confidant, a Doctor Pacek, who after careful study of church laws prepared a memorandum which concluded that marriage between second cousins was permissible. Eventually this memorandum was to be sent to the head of the Serbian church, but first a new ministry had to be formed. This task was entrusted to

Jovan Ristić, long Serbia's minister to Constantinople. Ristić proposed that all ministers be replaced except for the minister of war, Milivoje Blaznavac, who was for the marriage in any case. Ristić's plan was that in return for their approval of the marriage, Mihailo would agree to a liberalization of his regime. Mihailo viewed this as blackmail, and dismissed Ristić.

Although basically a middle of the road conservative, Ristić, by virtue of his stand, became the hero of the liberals. Although another ministry was chosen by the prince, Ristić seemed to be back in Mihailo's good graces within a short time. There were even signs that Mihailo, before he met his death on May 29 (Julian Calendar), 1868, was moving toward Ristić's views concerning the need for political reforms. He seems to have realized that the supporters of his despotic regime were opposed to his marriage, while those who would tolerate it were insistent on reforms.

The End of Mihailo's Reign

The plot to kill Mihailo and to take over the government was well-prepared. It was the work of a few individuals, most of whom suffered from personal disappointments or held grudges against Mihailo's regime. It was not the work of a political faction; the plotters simply believed that they would usher in a new regime which would not condemn them for getting rid of a despotic ruler.[28] They succeeded in killing Mihailo, but the failure of the killers to pass on the news soon enough to their co-conspirators enabled his ministers to learn of the assassination first and to take the necessary steps to prevent a seizure of power.

Mihailo had taken an evening walk in the forest next to Topčider park, which is some distance from the center of the city. He had done this many times before and usually without any guard. He had received anonymous letters urging him to be careful but he was not concerned. As a matter of fact, he had forbidden a secret service guard, not wishing to give the impression that he was afraid. On the fateful evening Mihailo was in the company of his love, Katarina, and her mother and grandmother. Of the two men who were along, only one was armed. The four assassins killed Katarina's mother, along with Mihailo, and wounded the other members of the party, except the grandmother, who was first out with the news.[29]

Ilija Garašanin was in Topčider park at the time and was one of the first to hear the sad news. Although no longer a minister, he hurried into Belgrade and called the ministerial council together and began giving orders. A temporary regency was established that same night, and four actions taken: (1) a proclamation that a Skupština would be called to decide on a new monarch, (2) a decree putting the army in an emergency status, (3) creation of summary courts to try the guilty, and (4) calling an election of a Large National Skupština for the purpose of choosing a prince.[30]

The next day, however, the minister of war, Blaznavac, decided the question of the prince in favor of Milan Obrenović, Mihailo's grand-nephew. Blaznavac ordered the army to swear allegiance to Milan, then a boy of 14 living in Paris. In this way, Blaznavac confronted the temporary regency with a *fait accompli*, a military coup, which they (and subsequently the Large National Skupština) could only ratify. A new regency was selected, consisting of Blaznavac, Jovan Ristić, and Jovan Gavrilović, none of whom was a member of the temporary regency.Moreover, no one of them was a recognized representative of past regimes.

According to Slobodan Jovanović: "Blaznavac was the first to successfully utilize the army for the solution of domestic political questions, and his example was contagious. . . . The history of Milan's son Alexander has beginning and ending chapters in an officers' conspiracy. . . . The Topčider catastrophe . . . announced the entry of the army into our internal politics."[31]

It is difficult to draw up a balance sheet on Mihailo's reign. Certainly, he is one of the most prominent of Serbia's rulers. He had vision, and his horizons were not narrow. There is some question, however, as to his ability and that of his ministers to pursue their goals. In the light of the conditions prevailing in Serbia at that time, Mihailo achieved much, although he was no doubt a frustrated man. He gave unstintingly of himself and his personal fortune. Unlike his father, who mixed with the people and whose residence was as open as any government office, Mihailo was reserved and more formal. He introduced pomp and ceremony at his court, and audiences had to be arranged for in advance. For the most part, he worked long hours, and associated almost exclusively with a narrow circle made up of his family and his ministers.

In the words of Slobodan Jovanović, Mihailo "was just, honest, noble; he had a high awareness of duty, much principle and steadfastness . . . patriotism . . . idealism. . . . But he . . . lacked a certain intellectual capacity that was required. . . . and he was indecisive."[32] But it should be noted that the Serbia of the 1860s was experiencing a time of political awakening, political parties were forming, and the people were beginning to demand a voice in public affairs. Whatever Mihailo's merits, it was clear that change was in the wind and could not long be postponed.

V. BEGINNINGS OF CONSTITUTIONALISM: CRITICAL DECADE, 1868-1878

The decade following the assassination of Prince Mihailo in 1868 witnessed several developments that were critical for the future of Serbian politics. The most important of these were: (1) the coming to the throne of a 14-year old monarch in whose name a regency ruled until he legally became of age on his 18th birthday; (2) the making of a full-fledged Serbian constitution by that regency; (3) the explicit recognition in practice of the principle of ministerial responsibility; (4) the conduct of two wars with Turkey; (5) the founding and organization of political parties (discussed in the next chapter). All of these developments played a role in shaping the beginnings of constitutional government in a decade of considerable uncertainty for Serbia.

The Monarch and the Regency

Because Mihailo had no direct heirs, his principal cabinet officers formed a temporary regency immediately following the assassination and called for the election of a constituent assembly (Large National Skupština) to select a new monarch. The minister of war, Milivoje Blaznavac, was not satisfied with this arrangement, and quickly proclaimed Milan Obrenović, Mihailo's 14-year old nephew then living in Paris, as the new prince of Serbia, and got the Belgrade garrison to swear allegiance to him. Blaznavac, who held the highest rank (colonel) in the Serbian army, had been in Paris at the time of the coup by Louis Napoleon and had become impressed with the power of bayonets in the hands of one daring enough to use them. When the Large National Skupština met it faced a *fait accompli*, and selected Blaznavac as first regent.

The politically moving force in the three-man regency was Jovan Ristić, who had been Serbia's representative in Constantinople from 1861 to 1867, and in the latter year was made minister of foreign affairs. Unlike most Serbian politicans, who up to that time were sons of civil servants, merchants, or well-to-do peasants, Ristić came from impoverished parents. As a bright young man, he studied in Germany with the aid of a government stipend, receiving a Ph.D. from Heidelberg. Subsequently, he spent two years at the Sorbonne in Paris. Although he took part in the Revolution of 1858, he was not identified in the 1860s with the young intelligentsia that was to form the Liberal party. Nevertheless he realized that a regime which became too unpopular could not survive. Consequently, he told Mihailo that political reforms were necessary, which resulted in his dismissal. This brought him popularity among the young liberals, and in the years following the reign of the regency he became the leader of the Liberal party.

A personal friend of Blaznavac, Ristić became a regent when he was only 38 years of age. Although cool and arrogant, he was respected and generally viewed as a superb statesman. As a moderate, he sought to combine a popular dynasty with notions of political freedom, so dear to the Liberals. The latter were receptive because of a dual fear—that they would be blamed for Mihailo's assassination and that the regency would take over their party. It is in this context that Ristić played the key role in the drafting and adoption of the Constitution of 1869.

In the early years of the regency, the young monarch did not present a problem, but he was learning fast. He developed a dislike for Blaznavac and Ristić because some of his friends and advisers told him that the 1869 constitution, which reduced his power, was in conflict with an earlier organic law that forbade changing the constitution during the minority of a monarch. Despite this, upon reaching age 18, Milan appointed Blaznavac prime minister and Ristić foreign minister. In addition, he made Blaznavac a general, the first one in Serbia. Ristić and Blaznavac might have clashed except for the fact that the latter died unexpectedly in March 1873, just as his star seemed to be rising.

By the time Milan was 19, he had well-formulated ideas about politics in Serbia. He saw the peasantry as incapable of governing; the civil service as demoralized; and no upper class which with the prince would be the carriers of the state idea (the larger property owners might become such a class but this would require decades). He noted that there was no bourgeoisie and no independent intelligentsia. He grasped the essence of political questions quickly, but he no doubt erred when he thought of himself as smarter than all of his ministers. A cynic at a young age, he did not believe in God, and looked upon all men as bad. For him all of life was a struggle in which the more clever and the more merciless won out.

In addition Milan early developed the habit of financial extravagance, which was to plague him during his lifetime. Moreover, he liked women and he did not attempt to hide his doings. Before reaching his twenty-first birthday he became engaged to Natalie Keśko, whose father was Russian and whose mother (like Milan's) was Rumanian. With the marriage a few months later (October 1875), however, his marital troubles were just beginning.

The Constitution of 1869

The Large National Skupština which ratified the choice of Milan as prince and the three regents, directed the regency to bring about certain political changes. The major ones were: an increase in the powers of the regular Skupština, freedom of the press, jury trials, and ministerial responsibility. In December 1868, the regency appointed a large committee of experts to consider a new constitution, and after some six months of deliberation, a draft was ready for ratification by a newly-elected Large National Skupština. The Council of State for a time resisted the trend of events, but after some pressure from the cabinet and the regency it yielded and elections for the Skupština were held on May 28, 1869. The Skupstina which met on June 10, 1869 numbered over 500 men, mainly peasants, with a few priests, merchants, and lawyers. After some arguments with the Council of State the constitution was adopted without detailed debate. There were a few amendments, including the defeat of the bicameral proviso in the draft and a change in the method of selecting Skupština officers.[1]

When the constitution was being drafted, the regency informed and consulted with Austria-Hungary and Russia. The former was in favor and the latter against constitutional change, but the Serbs assured the Russians that the reforms would be moderate. Turkey was not informed, but was confronted with a *fait accompli*. Nevertheless, the Turks accepted the constitution without protest.

Perhaps the most significant aspect of the constitution was the elevation of the National Skupština to the position of a real legislative body. It stated that the "legislative power is exercised by the National Skupština with the Prince." Then it provided that "no law can be promulgated, repealed, amended or reinterpreted without the agreeement of the National Skupština." In case of great internal or external dangers, decree powers could be exercised, but these actions would have to be ratified at a later date by the Skupština. In actual lawmaking, bills could emanate from the legislature or the executive, but the constitution gave cabinet measures priority. The Skupština was given control over finance, although it could not attach unrelated matters to finance bills, and in case of disagreement the existing budget could be extended by the monarch for one year if such an order carried the countersignature of all ministers.

Aside from acquiring legislative power, the Skupština became a fixed institution with regular annual meetings, and a provision for special sessions. Three-fourths of its members were to be elected, with suffrage extended to all males who paid a certain minimum in taxes (members of cooperatives were assumed to have paid the minimum). This came close to being universal manhood suffrage. The remaining one-fourth of the deputies were to be appointed by the prince, although he was not obligated to appoint his full quota. The need for the appointed deputies stemmed from the fact that the draft of the constitution made civil servants ineligible for election, to which the constituent assembly added lawyers. The only way that eminent men of scholarship or experience in public affairs could enter the Skupština, therefore, was by appointment. Moreover, the constitution explicitly stated that deputies are not the representatives of those who choose them, but of the whole people.

The prince's contacts with the Skupština, except on formal occasions, were to be carried out through his ministers. Ristić had concluded that there would never be domestic peace until political responsibility was transferred from the prince to the ministers.[2] In his speech to the Large National Skupština he said that the constitution had placed the prince above every struggle and hence he was non-responsible.[3] His powers to call and adjourn sessions of parliament, as well as to dissolve it and to call new elections, would presumably be exercised through his ministers. Moreover, his power to veto legislative enactments would presumably also be exercised on the basis of recommendations from his ministers.

The constitution said very little concerning the precise relationship between the prince and his ministers. It stated that the ministers were chosen and dismissed by the prince, and that they were responsible to him and to the National Skupština. Every act of his in state affairs had to be countersigned by the respective minister.

This suggests that ministerial responsibility was provided for, but other provisions of the constitution suggest that the framers were thinking in terms of legal rather than political responsibility. Ministers could not be members of the Skupština, but they could participate in parliamentary discussions and had the last word after other debate had ended. While there was no explicit provision for the resignation of ministers should they lose the confidence of the Skupština, the constitution did declare that ministers could be questioned and that they were obligated to furnish information. Moreover, there was a proviso that ministers could withdraw a measure any time prior to a final vote, perhaps a recognition of the importance of parliamentary views. Finally, the power to dissolve the Skupština would lead to some test of the public's reaction to the differences between the ministers and the legislature.

As a compromise document, the constitution left many persons dissatisfied, especially those who thought that the Skupština's powers had been limited in several respects. The failure of the constitution to be explicit about judicial independence, rights of local self-government, and guarantees concerning freedom of the press, speech and association (these were to be spelled out in legislative acts)—all added to the dissatisfaction. Yet in view of Serbia's past history, the Constitution of 1869 was a great step toward constitutional government. In any case, it provided the governmental machinery out of which parliamentary government could and did evolve.

The Recognition of Ministerial Responsibility

The reign of the regency under the new constitution (1869-1872) was a period of relative tranquility and also one of fear. One man, Radivoje Milojković (Liberal), headed the cabinet during the entire period. Under his premiership, with the aid and guidance of the regents, the government persecuted known Karadjordjević supporters, something that was not done prior to Mihailo's assassination. Moreover, fear was instilled in the populace with the execution of 17 men found guilty of being involved in the killing. In addition, pressure tactics were used in elections to keep potential opponents out of the Skupština. In essence, the regents reasoned that it was better to have some police terror than to have a new assassination.

On the other hand, government supporters were well-organized, while whatever opposition existed was unorganized and unready. Ministers were more clever than in the past; they permitted the deputies to talk and they listened. There were reasons for opposition: (1) partisanship (rewards for support); (2) nepotism (rule largely by two families); and (3) corruption (although not great). But the Skupština and the press did not go beyond the boundaries of moderation, and crises were avoided.

During the reign of the regency the government showed some concern with economic questions, but special emphasis was placed on education, partly because the government gave less in the areas of political freedom. A teachers' college was established in 1870, and better salaries for teachers were instituted. A forestry school was founded in 1870. Students were warned, however, against involvement in politics. The government's concern with economic questions was limited and without special direction. The budget was balanced largely because of special sources of income, and the first Serbian bank was founded. The need to build railroads was recognized, but the necessary capital could not be found.

When Milan became of age in 1872, he first appointed Milivoje Blaznavac and then Jovan Ristić as premier. Both men were identified with the Liberals. The former died in March 1873, and the latter, partly because he was unsuccessful in forming a ministry with Conservative leaders, resigned after heading a cabinet of civil servants for six months. Although short-lived, Ristić's cabinet had the distinction of being the first in Serbia where the ministers were appointed on the recommendation of the prime minister.[4] The only exception was the minister of war whom Milan appointed and who had to be personally loyal to him, a practice that remained under Milan and under his son Alexander.

Following Ristić's resignation, Milan appointed Jovan Marinović to head a cabinet of Conservatives, who a few years later adopted the name Progressive. Within three months a number of important new laws were enacted, among them laws designed to assist industrial enterprises, to protect a minimum acreage (12) of a peasant's land from being disposed of in any way (sale, tax, debt), to build prisons, to do away with corporal punishment, to adopt the metric system, to institute coinage of silver.[5] But Marinović is less well known for these laws than for the fact that he was the first Serbian prime minister to recognize explicitly that a cabinet could not stay in power if it did not have the confidence of the legislature. Under him ministerial responsibility became a fact of Serbian political life.

Marinović first posed the question of confidence to a somewhat bewildered special session of the Skupština in January 1874.[6] Although he derived some temporary satisfaction from the vote of confidence he won on this occasion, Marinović was aware of his cabinet's precarious position in a Skupština largely dominated by Liberals. Consequently, in the elections of October 1874, he sought victories for Conservative candidates. He did not succeed. Because Skupština deputies had not until that time separated into parties, he was not sure of the actual line-up of the deputies, and therefore decided to meet the new Skupština. After a two-day debate on what should go into the address in answer to the speech from the throne, Marinović realized that his was the minority position. In the actual vote, the cabinet's proposal won by a vote of 61 to 58, with three absentions. Marinović interpreted this victory as an actual defeat, and the ministers resigned. In this we have the fall of the first Serbian cabinet as a result of an adverse vote in the Skupština.

In explaining the cabinet's resignation to the Skupština, Marinović said:

> A majority of three votes. . . is so weak that the ministry cannot have the slightest hope. . . . After such a great discussion of the matter, where the ministry had the greatest hope of convincing you as to the correctness of its ideas, it makes it impossible to carry out its duties. . . I consider it a duty to inform you that following the outcome of yesterday's voting, the ministry has resigned.[7]

Following Marinović's fall, his minister of interior, Aćim Čumić, formed a new cabinet, a coalition of sorts that included a leader of the Liberal opposition. The new cabinet lasted less than two months. It simply disintegrated. It was snowed under with interpellations—some thirty of them. Instead of answering them, Čumić put the question of confidence first, and although he received a favorable vote each time, some of the ministers were opposed to this practice. Several of them resigned after he had again put the question of confidence without consulting them.[8] Thereupon Čumić submitted the resignation of the whole cabinet, a recognition of the collective responsibility of the whole cabinet.

After an unsuccessful attempt to get Jevrem Grujić, the leader of the Liberals, to form a cabinet (his proposed list of ministers was unaceptable to the monarch), Milan entrusted the formation of a new ministry to Danilo Stefanović, a Conservative. Ostensibly a "ministry of conciliation and good will," it came into office in January, 1875, but soon experienced difficulties. It called for new elections in August 1875, and resigned the day after the elections in which the Liberals had won a majority. The Liberals, who were identified as anti-Turkish, were aided in their victory by the fact that a revolt of Serbs in Bosnia-Hercegovina had broken out in July.

While subsequent ministries also recognized that they could stay in office only if they had the support of the majority in the Skupština, Jovan Ristić stated it best. In a six-day debate on the address in November 1879, he staked his political life on the outcome. Although probably confident of his majority, he took an energetic part in the discussion. Among other things, he said:

I am not afraid of a lack of confidence. It could do nothing to
my past, and it is not at all dishonorable to fall in parliament. In
constitutional states, governments do not fall except in parliament.
It is not good where it happens otherwise. . . . I am confident
that the minority will remain and that the majority will do justice
to whom it belongs. For that reason, I propose that in the name
of the government . . . that there be a roll-call vote.[9]

The roll-call vote was favorable to the cabinet (113 to 35, with one
abstention), but Ristić's opposition continued to be vocal, and he
again had an opportunity to lecture the deputies on the meaning of
parliamentary government.[10]

Serbian Politics and Wars with Turkey

Following the defeat at the polls of the Stefanović ministry in
August 1875, there was some turmoil before a new cabinet could be
formed. Centrally involved was the question of whether Serbia could
assist the uprising of her compatriots in Bosnia-Hercegovina, and
thereby very likely get involved in a war with Turkey. The Liberals
were the war party, but Milan and the Conservatives were opposed.
Milan did not think that Serbia could succeed, and the Great Powers
advised noninvolvement. The press and the public, however, were
for war. After considerable difficulties and two acting or transitional
cabinets, Milan became convinced that war was unavoidable. Thereupon, in April 1876 he entrusted the formation of a new cabinet to
the Liberals. Stevča Mihailović was made premier, and Jovan Ristić
minister of foreign affairs and "if need be" deputy premier.

The coming to power of this ministry was in conformity with
the secret actions of the Skupština of the previous September. Left
by the prince and the cabinet to make the decision, the Skupština
had voted 77 to 30, with five abstentions, to assist the uprising. Also
in a secret vote, it had approved a loan of 3 million ducats by a vote
of 67 to 39, with four abstentions.[11] The voting was not along party
lines but in accordance with personal convictions. Following these
votes Milan precipitated a resignation of the newly installed cabinet.
After considerable difficulty a transitional ministry, under the leadership of Ljubomir Kaljević (Liberal) was formed. Interestingly enough,
it concerned itself mainly with domestic affairs, increasing the powers
of local government and lessening the powers of the police.[12] Following his resignation in April 1876, the Mihailović-Ristić war cabinet,
referred to in the previous paragraph, came into being.

War was declared in June 1876 by Serbia (population 1.5 million), against Turkey (population 40 million), partly because of the

urgings of unofficial Russia. General Michael Cherniaev was the spokesman of this unofficial Russia. He came with nearly 3,000 Russian volunteers, but the ill-prepared and inexperienced Serbian forces were being beaten when at the insistence of the Great Powers an armistice was reached in October. A shaky peace was concluded in February 1877, and in December the Serbs went to war with Turkey a second time, this time at the urgings of official Russia. The war ended in January 1878, with Turkey's defeat.

In anticipation of the signing of the peace to end the first war in February 1877, Milan exerted pressure on his cabinet to agree to the election of a Large National Skupština. The war had been hard on the Serbian peasants; the people had borne four-fifths of the cost, mainly through government requisitions.[13] Milan wanted to saddle the Liberals with the responsibility for the war, but the composition of the Large National Skupština did not give him much hope. Therefore, he adjourned it as soon as it had approved the terms for peace.

The second war ended on a bitterly disappointing note for Serbia. Although the Serbs had fought side by side with the Russians, the latter signed the Peace of San Stefano with Turkey without Serbian participation. Moreover, Russia treated Serbia almost as an enemy, creating a Great Bulgaria at the expense of Serbian-populated areas, some of which Serbian forces had liberated. Particularly since Bulgaria had not participated in the war, the Serbs asked for an explantion. They were cynically told that Russian interests came first, then Bulgarian, and only third Serbian interests.[14] Although much of San Stefano was undone at the Congress of Berlin in 1878, with Serbia gaining about 200 square miles of territory, the Russians had added insult to injury by promising to Austria-Hungary the occupation of Bosnia-Hercegovina, and without telling the Serbs of what they had done. It is understandable, therefore, that Milan, who in the first half of his reign was under Russia's influence, should become her sworn enemy in the second half.

In large measure because of his effective work at the Congress of Berlin, Jovan Ristić was made prime minister in September 1878. One of his first acts was to order new elections in October, which the Liberals won. At the same time, a coherent opposition group of 40 deputies (out of 172) came into existence, which was the nucleus of the Radical party soon to be founded. At the second session of the Skupština in November 1879, the opposition candidate for the presidency of parliament received 71 votes. The position of the Ristić cabinet became shaky, partly because the opposition became more daring and partly because Ristić's popularity had declined, principally

because of difficult postwar problems. In October 1880, the Ristić
cabinet fell, not because of an adverse vote in the Skupština but
because Ristić resigned when he could not go along with Milan in
policies which would make Serbia economically dependent upon
Austria-Hungary.[15]

The Ristić cabinet had been the culmination of Liberal party
rule. His fall was also the fall of the Liberal party as a ruling party.
It was also the beginning of Milan's swimming in anti-parliamentary
waters. Although Ristić was one of Serbia's greatest statesmen in
the 19th century, he did not seek favor with the palace nor did he
have an inclination to lead the masses. What he succeeded in doing
in the critical decade can be attributed in large part to the fact that
both the monarch and Serbian democracy were young.[16]

In large part because of his tutelage in the critical decade Serbia
made significant progress toward constitutional government. While
the newly-born constitution left much to be desired, it proved work-
able, even in extremely difficult circumstances, because most of
those entrusted with leadership understood its spirit as well as its
limitations. By 1880, however, the leaders of the emerging Radical
party (as well as some others) were determined that the people's
representatives in the Skupština should be the dominant force in
Serbian politics. At the same time, Prince Milan was convinced that
the monarch's powers were being eroded, a development he did not
cherish and which he increasingly resisted, leading to a serious con-
frontation. To better understand the political forces at work, it is
necessary to turn our attention to the growth and formation of
Serbian political parties.

POLITICAL PARTIES AND ELECTIONS

Political parties, as well-defined groups or movements, came into existence in Serbia only in the 1870s.[1] Formal organization of parties with written programs began about 1880. Groups struggling for power (or seeking limits on the power of others), however, were in evidence much earlier. They began with Serbia's first successful revolution in 1804. The early struggles, under both Karadjordje and Miloš, cannot be defined clearly in class or ideological terms, although they left their mark in the form of specific political institutions. In the late 1830s, however, certain well-to-do merchants and high civil and military functionaries succeeded in limiting Miloš through the creation of a Council, which in fact became stronger than Miloš, and forced his abdication. This was the beginning of the twenty-year rule of the oligarchy known as the Defenders of the Constitution regime.

In a sense the oligarchy was government by and for the bureaucrats and their friends. The leaders of the oligarchy who unseated Miloš were men who had held high military and bureaucratic posts. They employed democratic phraseology but they were not democrats. They and their collaborators wanted to be able to engage in free trade without permits, most of which were in the hands of Miloš's relatives and friends. In addition to the demand for free trade, they also sought guarantees for private property and legal security, as well as prestige for the bureaucracy. The latter gained positions and privileges, during the rule of the oligarchy, it had never enjoyed before or since. There were titles, ranks, uniforms, and they paid little or no tax. Civil servants engaged in profitable trade, which was forbidden in 1848, but continued to a degree thereafter in spite of the prohibition. It was the isolation of the oligarchy from the people and the abuses and indifference of its bureaucracy that brought an end to their regime in 1858.

As we look at the political groups and movements of the 1860s and 1870s that were to become the principal political parties in Serbia, we also need to keep in mind that throughout the 19th century many Serbs found themselves the uncompromising adherents of one or the other dynasty—Obrenović or Karadjordjević. Miloš had ordered the murder of Karadjordje, and on the abdication of Miloš and his son Mihailo after 1838, Karadjordje's son Alexander became prince, only to see himself ousted in 1858 and the return of Miloš and Mihailo. The latter's assassination in 1868 was thought to have been the work of Karadjordjević partisans, who were persecuted in the ensuing years. Mihailo's successors, Milan and his son Alexander, tended to identify their political opponents with the supporters of Peter Karadjordjević, which was only partially true. The obliteration of the Obrenović dynasty in 1903, and the installation of Peter Karadjordjević as king, ended the dynastic struggle. But some observers have pointed out that the struggles of the partisans of the two dynasties throughout the 19th century were in a sense akin to struggles between political parties. The principal parties were perceived by a large part of the public as being identified with one or the other dynasty—the Liberals and Progressives as pro-Obrenović and the Radicals as pro-Karadjordjević.

The Liberal Party

During the rule of the oligarchy educated men were respected, and the regime sent a modest number of promising young scholars to study in Western European universities. Upon their return, however, it was evident that they had become imbued with liberal ideas, and soon were the articulate critics of the existing system. These liberal intellectuals, the nucleus of the future Liberal party, were first recognized as a political force when they combined with Obrenović partisans in the Saint Andrew's Skupština of 1858 to carry out a bloodless revolution against the Defenders of the Constitution and against the prince, Alexander Karadjordjević. At that Skupština, the young liberal intellectuals provided much of the leadership. They were the best prepared, the most educated, the most active, and the most aggressive.[2]

Unhappy with Mihailo's autocratic rule, the liberals could do little inside Serbia during his reign. Since public meetings and political newspapers were not permitted, they did most of their agitating orally among the people at fairs and expositions. Their like-minded compatriots abroad were active, however, publishing newspapers in Geneva, Budapest, and Novi Sad, which were critical of Mihailo's regime. Some of these found their way into Serbia. During a large part of Mihailo's reign, Jovan Ristić, Serbia's leading statesman at the time, was a broker between the Prince and the liberal leaders. Toward the end of Mihailo's regime, as Ristić began pressing Mihailo for liberal reforms, he attracted liberal support and in fact became the leader of what at best could be said to be a loosely organized Liberal party. As the politically dominant force in the regency after

Mihailo's assassination, Ristić was a strong Obrenović partisan. Liberals accepted support for the dynasty, but they expected much more from Ristić and from themselves.

Perhaps more than anything else, the Liberal party demanded annual meetings of the Skupština. They insisted that it was the "oldest, most significant, and most sacred Serbian institution." In their arguments they even harked back to the ecclesiastical assemblies of medieval Serbia. They wanted the Skupština to have real legislative power, and they believed that ministers should be responsible to it. To achieve this type of Skupština, the Liberals demanded a free press. In addition, they cultivated the cult of education, believing that an educated people would not tolerate tyranny.

Moreover, the Liberals were uncompromising nationalists. Concern for their compatriots still under foreign rule was high on their political agenda, a concern which led them to two wars against Turkey, discussed in the previous chapter. They hated all symbols of Turkish influence in Serbia, and especially the ever-present fez, and worked to eradicate them.

The Liberals were unhappy with the Constitution of 1869, because it embodied their program only in part. The Skupština's legislative power was limited, and provision for ministerial responsibility and a free press left much to be desired. Nevertheless, the Liberals were in power under this constitution for nearly ten years.

During their rule in the 1870s, the Liberals did not have much in the way of party organization. To a large extent the government bureaucracy served as the party's office staff. Only in 1880 did the party formulate an organizational statute, with local committees and the Main Committee. In 1881 the party published a formal program which emphasized preservation of political freedoms at home and unification with Serbia of Serbs under foreign rule. A new party statue in 1883 made the party organization more democratic, and a new program in 1888 appeared to emulate the successful Radical party. But new promises and new programs (1892-1893) did not bring new members.

By the time that the Liberal party began to organize seriously, the Radical party had caught the imagination of the peasant masses, with the result that between 1880 and 1887 the Liberals had only 7 to 15 deputies in parliament. At one time they had had a fair amount of peasant support, although its parliamentary deputies and party organization people were mainly merchants with some lawyers and peasants. Many of its active and influential supporters were civil servants, as well as many of the higher clergy. Although it continued to hope, the party had pretty well played out its role on the historical scene by 1880.

The Progressive Party

The Progressive party sprang from the group of young conservatives, imbued with Western liberal ideas, whose basic program was "Law, freedom, progress." They were joined by a few one-time Liberals, and in the main their social composition was akin to that of the Liberals. They were led by a few leading intellectuals, but they never managed to put down roots among the masses. Two of their early leaders were Jovan Marinović and Aćim Čumić, who briefly headed ministries in 1873-1875. Their better known leaders were Milan Piroćanac, Čedomil Mijatović, Stojan Novaković, and Milutin Garašanin (son of Ilija Garašanin of the oligarchy regime). The latter was their real leader.

The Progressives came into their own in 1880, and stayed in power for seven years. They had eclipsed the Liberals party because of the high costs of the two wars with Turkey and because of the Liberals' inclination toward a tariff war with Austria-Hungary, which business interests did not want. But just as they got to power, the newly-founded Radical party captured the support of the peasantry. Without roots among the people, the Progressives allied themselves with the palace, and in fact became King Milan's personal party, and when he fell they also tumbled.

They did establish a democratic organizational structure with a card-carrying membership. In 1881 and in more detailed provisions in 1889, local and area committees were set up, as well as annual party congresses, and the Main Committee of 30 (in the capital) was elected by the congress. The top leaders, however, did not maintain close connections with organizational leaders below, and when they did it was in the cities and not in the peasant areas. Moreover, they did not pay much attention to agitation and propaganda. And they did not have the fiery orators that the Radicals were blessed with, nor did their democratic organization attract a significant number of voters.

In power, however, the Progressives promulgated important reforms. If we put aside for the moment the fact that they became the tools of Milan in putting down the Radical rebellion (Timočka buna) in 1883, we must recognize the progressive measures they enacted.[3] They were motivated by the desire to modernize and Europeanize

Serbia, to transform a patriarchal country into a contemporary European state. Among the laws passed were those dealing with freedom of speech and press, judicial independence, freedom of association and organization, free elections, compulsory education, and reforms in local government and taxation. In addition, they launched the building of railroads, and they established a national standing army.

The fate of the Progressives was closely tied to King Milan's fate. His problems were their problems, as the next chapter will show. In the beginning they were a party of a free-thinking Western intelligentsia. The appearance of the Radical party, however, derailed them. In their eyes the "despotism of the masses" became a greater danger than the despotism of the monarch. Never having had strong roots among the people, they rapidly became a palace camarilla. When their patron abdicated in 1889, they ceased to be a significant force in the politics of Serbia.

The Radical Party

The ideological father of the Serbian National Radical party was the socialist, Svetozar Markovic, but he died in 1875 at the age of 27 and before the party was organized.[4] The budding movement fell under the influence of the more practical bent of his followers. Initially, two brilliant publicists (Adam Bogosavljević and Pera Todorović) took most of Markovic's ideas to the peasant masses, but they were careful to avoid mentioning the socialist ideas that would have been repugnant to the peasants. They emphasized Marković's attack on the bureaucracy and his call for organizing the nation politically on the principle of self-government. Moreover, they championed his call for guaranteeing all basic political rights and his demand that ministers be responsible to the Skupština. In essence they were propagating for a type of peasant state—for peasant sovereignty.

The real founder of the Radical party was Nikola Pašić, who determined its ideological and organizational cast, and who was to be its leader (with brief interruptions) until his death in 1926.[5] He was the first among the Radicals to be elected to the Skupština in 1878, and in 1880 he organized the opposition deputies into a coherent caucus, the first to be formed in Serbia. In the latter year a party program was worked out, and published in the newly-founded party newspaper, *Samouprava* (self-government), in January 1881. Moreover, party statutes were worked out and the first national congress was held in 1882, at which Pašić was selected president without opposition. At that time he said that "the states which reached the highest degree of enlightenment were those in which the people ruled," and therefore it was necessary to change the constitution "in the spirit of democratic freedoms, in the spirit of people's sovereignty, in the spirit of people's self-government."

In general the Radicals could speak the language of the peasants. The following is a sample, almost word for word, of their ability to put things in ways easily understood by the peasants: People without a constitution are like nomads who live on the bare ground under an outstretched canvas; people with a bad constitution are like men who live in small and miserable thatched huts which are full of smoke, darkness, cold, and dirt; people with a good constitution are like men who have large and well-lighted rooms in which all live in warmth and comfort. The ability to talk in these terms to largely illiterate peasants quickly secured for the Radicals a large and enthusiastic following.

The party's program, dealing almost exclusively with domestic affairs, stressed the need of amending the constitution so that the Skupština would be freely elected by all adult citizens, that it have full legislative power, and that it meet annually on a specified date. Moreover, the program demanded reforms in the bureaucracy which would make administration simple, cheap, effective, and that it respect local self-government. In addition, the program called for a direct and progressive income tax, educational opportunities for all, and for economic improvements. In foreign affairs, the program stressed the need to liberate the still subjugated parts of Serbdom, to strive for closer relations with Montenegro and Bulgaria, and to strengthen the national army (a type of people's militia), leaving the standing army the principal task of training the national army. Before the constitution could be amended to achieve some of the above-mentioned objectives, the program demanded legislation to guarantee freedom of speech and press, freedom of association, recognition of communal self-government, and security for persons and property. Finally, the program created the party organ, *Samouprava*.

Under Pašić's guidance, the Radical party was the first political party in Serbia to organize systematically. Moreover, Pašić made it a highly disciplined party, with the rank and file expected to support the leadership. The most important policy-making body was the Main Committee, consisting of the principal party leaders in Belgrade. When the Skupština was in session, however, the caucus of the party's deputies was more powerful. From time to time, when the leader believed it necessary in the consideration of some problem, the Main

Committee was augmented with district leaders from the interior. There were annual national congresses but these were not policy-making bodies. The party also had regional and local committees. In all of these party bodies democratic procedures were to be followed, but party policies were rarely debated, and comments were really in the form of information for the policy makers. In practice, however, the party was often less disciplined than it seemed.

Although the party statute provided for a dues-paying member-ship, success was instantaneous. Within less than two years the party had over 45,000 enrolled members,[6] with at least that many more who were unenrolled. Initially, the membership was made up mainly of peasants, with teachers and priests in the role of leaders, but the party soon began to attract vocal intellectuals—literary figures and professors. The party became attractive also to merchants who liked the idea that government should cost less. Moreover, the party experienced unbelievable and immediate successes at the polls as the next chapter will show. These instantaneous successes may also have contributed to the Timok rebellion in 1883, following which the party was severely repressed and many of its leaders shot or persecuted. But the people's loyalty and attachment to the party could not be destroyed.

The widespread and overwhelming successes of the Radicals also served to discourage the formation of minor parties. A few of Svetozar Marković's ideological followers, however, sought (unsuccessfully) to organize a socialist party in 1881, believing that the Radicals had abandoned Marković's basic ideas. Ultimately, of course, a socialist party was bound to be organized. In 1903, under the leadership of Dimitrije Tucović and Radovan Dragović, the Serbian Social-Democratic party was formed. They did not attract many followers.

Political Mobilization and Elections

Communicating political ideas and mobilizing support for political programs or movements in any systematic way was not much in evidence in Serbia until the 1870s. To a degree it was done before that time by the prince, by Orthodox church leaders, and by the few educated people, but it was not systematized and it was in the main in the form of oral discussion. At the same time, oral communication should not be minimized, because for decades, even after the printing of newspapers, a largely illiterate population was educated politically in this way. Serbian peasants seemed to have had an extraordinary interest in and liking for politics. Even if they could not read or write, they listened to discussions, asked questions, and expressed themselves. With the expansion of formal education and the coming into existence of newspapers, it became possible for the expression of political opinions to be more widely shared, and for political alternatives to be brought into sharper focus.

As the political parties developed, it became accepted practice that each party have at least one known organ, usually a newspaper.[7] Some parties also printed periodicals and political tracts. In the case of the Radicals, Svetozar Marković and his colleagues put out newspapers several years before the formal founding of their party. These were banned after publishing for a few months, partly because they had defended the Paris Commune. So long as the socialist press limited itself to economic questions, however, it was left alone.[8] The initial press laws under the 1869 Constitution provided for a relatively free press, and many new newspapers came into being, although several failed for economic reasons. At times newspapers did not dare to print certain things, but at the same time they could complain that the press was not free. Moreover, there were times when the cabinet in power had no newspaper, while the opposition had several. When the press laws were altered to make censorship and the banning of papers easier, several satirical publications came into existence, and they enjoyed considerable success. Press laws were changed several times in the latter decades of the 19th century, sometimes in favor of greater freedom and at other times in the form of greater restrictions.

As time moved on, in addition to the partisan press, the number of publications about politics increased rapidly. Some of these were original studies and some were translations of Western European authors.[9] For a long time, the content of Serbian publications was weighted heavily in terms of the needs for a freely elected Skupština, responsibility of ministers, security of political liberties, and issues of national independence. As these issues were in the process of being resolved, particularly after 1869, political party struggles tended to concentrate on the question of control of government jobs, foreign debts, foreign control of the salt monopoly, and subsequently the foreign ownership and operation of the railroads, and Austria-Hungary's economic exploitation of the state.

With the establishment throughout the peasant areas of local party committees by the Radicals, political communication and mobilization took on a personal aspect. The people were told not only about the party's ideas and programs, but in addition were instructed concerning their electoral rights and what to do if these rights were infringed. In addition, visits by national leaders and the organization of political rallies made election campaigns more meaningful and more dramatic. Other parties sought to emulate the Radicals, but their successes were indeed limited by comparison.

Although there were no electoral laws prior to the adoption of the Constitution of 1869, the really significant ones for this study are those of 1870 and 1890.[10] The 1870 law provided that electors had to be 21 years of age and that they pay some amount in direct taxes. Because the latter provision was somewhat vague and subject to varying interpretations, Serbia approached universal manhood suffrage. Lists of eligible voters were posted in advance of elections, and appeals could be made by persons who believed themselves eligible. Voting was direct in the cities and indirect in the peasant areas, and it was public. To qualify as a candidate for the Skupština one had to have reached the age of 30, and to have paid a higher direct tax than was required of electors.

The 1890 electoral law followed from the Constitution of 1888. It provided that an elector needed to pay 15 dinars of direct tax, but because members of cooperatives *(zadruge)* were assumed to have paid at least that much by virtue of tax payments made by the cooperatives, Serbia approached universal manhood suffrage. As cooperative membership dwindled in subsequent years, however, a significant number of Serbs was disenfranchised by 1912. Secret voting, through the use of small rubber balls, was introduced by the electoral law of 1890. It also provided for direct election of deputies in the cities, with a runoff if no candidate received an absolute majority of the votes cast. In the peasant areas several deputies were elected from a single electoral district, and these were apportioned to party lists on the basis of proportional representation.[11] A specific date was set for elections, and provision was made for elections to fill vacancies as well as in the event of a dissolution of the Skupština.

In order to be eligible as a candidate under the 1890 law, a person had to have reached age 30, and to have paid 30 dinars in direct taxes. Unlike the 1870 law, however, the 1890 statute made civil servants (except those in police administration) eligible, but if elected and seated they would lose their positions in the bureaucracy. Those who had recently retired from police administration could not be candidates in the city or district where they served unless they had left the service at least 30 days prior to the date of the decree calling for new elections.[12] Soldiers and active officers could neither be candidates nor voters. In order that some of the more educated persons get on the list of candidates, there was a proviso that each list of candidates must have at least two persons on it who had a university education or had completed a technical education of comparable order.

The electoral law which followed the 1903 constitution was closely patterned after that of 1890.

Some Serbian elections were free and others subject to a good deal of governmental pressure. Prior to the broad awakening of the people by the political parties (i.e., prior to 1880), the cabinet in power could pretty much get the results that it desired. The general tendency was toward freer elections, but there were setbacks. The elections of 1870 and 1874 were accompanied by a good deal of police pressure. Those in 1875, 1877, 1878, and 1880 were relatively free. The elections of 1883, the first with organized parties so that it was known to which party each candidate belonged, were the most free up to that time. But because the results were so unacceptable to King Milan and his close associates, the resulting Skupština was adjourned as soon as it met. In the elections of 1886 and 1887, there was considerable police pressure, but those in 1888 and 1889 were fully free.

The electoral law of 1890 placed an independent government organ, usually a lawyer or a judge, to oversee elections and to guarantee that they were conducted freely. The first elections under this law (in 1893) were completely free, but in 1894 the electoral law of 1870 was brought back, with all its shortcomings, and with two subsequent elections being something less than free. Nevertheless, the elections of 1897 were relatively free, and with the return in 1903 of the Constitution of 1888 and the electoral law of 1890, with minor modifications in both, Serbian elections again became fully free and remained so thereafter. There were complaints, however, that under the proportional representation system certain parties did not get a fair share of Skupština seats in the 1903 to 1914 period.[13]

Because of widespread illiteracy, voting in Serbian elections was with little rubber balls. Secrecy was preserved by having the voter place his hand in each party box, and then depositing the ball in the box of his choice.

MILAN OBRENOVIĆ VS. THE RADICAL PARTY

Milan began the second half of his reign with a determination that he was not going to govern with the Liberals, mainly because their leader, Jovan Ristić, had not hesitated to disagree with the monarch. When Ristić resigned after one of their disagreements Milan turned to the Progressive party, which was blessed with some gifted leaders who were initially referred to as "young conservatives." Unfortunately for Milan and for them, the Progressive party never won a significant popular following, primarily because just as they came to power the newly-founded Radical party captured the peasant masses. Nevertheless Milan kept the Progressives in power for seven years despite the fact that their party was the smallest of the three. In the end, however, he not only gave way to the Radical majority, but in addition presided over the making of a truly democratic constitution, abdicated his throne in favor of his 13 year old son, and brought back Jovan Ristić to be the principal regent, the same Ristić who had been regent during Milan's own minority twenty years earlier.

First Years of Progressive Rule

Milan entrusted the formation of the first Progressive cabinet to Milan S. Piroćanac in October 1880. New elections held soon thereafter brought mainly Progressives and a loose association of Radicals to the Skupština. Because the Radicals were also hostile toward the Liberals, they cooperated for a time with the new cabinet. This was especially true while the Progressives were working on the enactment of laws concerning freedom of the press, association, and meetings. Milan was not too happy about these laws, but he found the Progressives indispensable because for the most part they were willing to follow his dictates, especially in foreign policy. They cooperated with Milan in ousting the head of the Serbian Orthodox church, Metropolitan Mihailo, and in supporting his secret treaty of June 1881 with Vienna, which in effect made Serbia an economic and political vassal of Austria-Hungary.[1] The precise contents of the treaty were known only to two or three Progressive leaders.

Despite an auspicious beginning, the Progressives were soon in trouble. The ouster of Metropolitan Mihailo and several bishops was not popular. Even more unpopular were the large-scale ousters, transfers, and promotions in the civil service to the benefit of Progressive partisans.[2] Moreover, the Radicals soon formed their own parliamentary caucus, and were ready to do battle when an appropriate opportunity arrived, which was not slow in coming. In January 1882 it became known that the Société de l'Union Générale, with whom the Progressives had concluded a loan for the building of railroads, as well as agreements for the building and exploitation of the railroads, had gone bankrupt.

There was an understandable concern as to the consequences for Serbia of this bankruptcy, but the cabinet did not dare meet the Skupština. Instead it took diversionary action. In February Serbia was proclaimed a kingdom and Milan king. This sudden and unanticipated proclamation was apparently taken so as to minimize the impact on the public of the consequences of the bankruptcy. But the Progressives' parliamentary difficulties were not overcome thereby. It soon became common knowledge that the borrowed money was left with l'Union Générale to draw interest, with the consequences that Serbia's loss would more than exceed its total annual governmental budget.[3]

In March 1882, after unsuccessful efforts to get at the truth through interpellations, 53 deputies (51 Radicals and 2 Liberals) resigned, leaving the Skupština without a quorum, which at that time was three-fourths of all deputies. The Radicals believed that their resignations would force new elections. The Progressive answer, however, was to get the Skupština officers to accept these resignations and to call for special elections to fill only the vacated posts.

The Progressives hoped to elect at least 12 deputies in the special elections which would ensure a quorum. King Milan, no longer even pretending to behave as a constitutional monarch, travelled throughout Serbia for a whole month, engaging in anti-Radical agitation. Nevertheless success eluded him and the Progressives. The latter won only 5 contests and the Radicals 45. The Radical deputies again resigned, whereupon the Piroćanac cabinet resigned, but Milan refused to accept their resignation.

Again new special elections were held to fill the vacated seats, but with the proviso that if the voters again voted for those who had resigned, these votes would not be counted. Instead those receiving the next highest vote would be declared elected.[4] In this way, some men entered the Skupština with no more than a handful of votes, some as low as 2 votes (Serbia at that time had indirect voting in rural areas). Those elected in this manner came to be referred to as "two votes," but the Skupština got its quorum. About 10 Radicals were elected since no votes were cast for any one else for those seats.

No one in the Progressive party believed in the legality of such elections. Consequently, Pirocánac and his colleagues again tried to resign, but were prevailed upon to stay by King Milan and the Austrian minister. With the help of the "two votes" the cabinet enacted several measures aimed at the Radicals, such as limiting freedom of the press and introducing a heavy monetary fine for absence from the Skupština which was aimed at denying it a quorum. In addition, some important laws were also passed, providing for (1) compulsory elementary school attendance, (2) the establishment of a standing army, (3) the setting up of a national bank, and (4) the creation of rules governing church authorities.

Pirocánac stayed on because Milan could find no other alternative. For a time Milan toyed with the idea of a "putsch," but got no support for it either inside or outside Serbia. What began as a struggle between the Progressives and the Radicals turned into a struggle between the king and the people. Prior to new elections that were to take place in 1883, further actions were taken against the Radicals, including the dismissal of their sympathizers in the civil service (including teachers) and the banning of the opposition press.

Radical Electoral Victories and the Timok Rebellion

The elections held in September were a disaster for Milan and the Progressives. The Radicals elected 61 deputies and the Progressives 34, with the Liberals getting 11, and 7 without party affiliation.[5] Aside from the matters mentioned above, the Radicals were apparently aided by allegations, substantially true, that in seeking the agreements with Serbia, l'Union Générale had spent money in attempts to bribe Serbian politicians. This was done with the apparent knowledge and sympathy of Milan. His prime minister, Pirocánac, at the very least permitted himself to get into a serious conflict of interest.[6]

Soon after the elections the Pirocánac cabinet resigned, but the king did not turn to the majority party. Instead, he appointed a cabinet of bureaucrats, headed by the arch conservative Nikola Hristić. Neither he nor King Milan wanted to have anything to do with the Radical Skupština. It was opened with one decree and then adjourned

with another, all in a matter of ten minutes. This slap in the face to
the victors left everyone wondering what would come next. It seems
that each side was waiting for the other to make the first move, the
significant difference being that the Radicals waited unprepared for
combat while Milan waited with the proverbial cocked pistol in hand.
The Radicals speculated on what the government might do, with the
most frequent guess being that the constitution would be abolished,
and that perhaps the members of the Radical Main Committee might
be arrested.

While both sides waited a rebellion broke out in the Timok
region of eastern Serbia,[7] where the Radicals were especially strong.
The immediate cause was the government's collection of national
militia firearms that had been left in the hands of the people. This
action, which could not have come at a worse psychological moment,
had been foreseen earlier when the Progressives created the standing
army but it had not been implemented. An article in the Radical
party organ, written during the summer of 1883 by the party leader,
Nikola Pašić, had discussed the disarming of the peasants, but his
advice was contradictory. On the one hand, he advised them to give
up their arms if they had to, but at the same time he said that they
should not leave their homes without arms. In any case, when the
rebellion broke out, the leaders in Belgrade were unprepared. After
one or two hurried and clandestine meetings of the party's Main
Committee, Pašić quietly crossed into Austria-Hungary, and travelled
to Rumania, avowedly determined to join the rebellion. Before he
could reach Serbian territory, however, he received word that the rebellion had already been put down. For the next six years he lived
in exile, mainly in Bulgaria.

The government's action against Radical leaders was swift and
brutal. A state of emergency was proclaimed and the standing army
was sent after the rebels. A summary court, established to try the
offenders, sentenced 94 to death and over 600 to varying prison
terms. Of the former, 20 were executed, among them Radical deputies, priests, and teachers. In addition, the members of the Radical
Main Committee were also tried, although legal evidence against
them was lacking, and three of them were sentenced to death, including Pašić who was tried in absentia. The sentences of the other two
were reduced to 10 years imprisonment. Two other members were
sentenced to 5 and 7 years respectively, while the remaining members were found innocent.

After the suppression of the Radicals, the Skupština was dissolved and new elections were held in January 1884. Except for

some 30 nondescript oppositionists, the whole Skupština was made up of government supporters. Nonetheless, the deputies wanted the cabinet to consult with them, something which did not come easy to the veteran bureaucrat Nikola Hristić, who soon resigned as prime minister. Milan then turned to the man who was soon to become the leader of the Progressive party, Milutin Garašanin, whose cabinet succeeded in getting enacted several laws that strengthened the position of the central authorities at the expense of local self-government and political freedom generally. In addition, several other measures were passed which were designed to put Serbia's finances in order.[8]

Milan's Troubles

Milan might have been able to continue ruling with the Progressives, even though they increasingly represented fewer and fewer citizens, if it had not been for certain critical problems. The major ones were (1) the disastrous war with Bulgaria (1885) and its consequences, (2) his difficulties with his wife Natalie, and (3) the differences that developed between him and his ministers. These problems, in combination, constituted overwhelming difficulties for Milan, which can be treated here only in the briefest form.

The war with Bulgaria was precipitated by Bulgaria's occupation of Eastern Rumelia in early September 1885, which Milan viewed as a violation of the Treaty of Berlin (1878), which had prevented the creation of a Great Bulgaria.[9] After it became evident that the Great Powers would do nothing except to agree that Bulgaria's action constituted a violation of the Treaty of Berlin, Milan declared war on November 2nd. Unprepared diplomatically, financially, or militarily, Serbia suffered a defeat, and accepted a peace which in the main was imposed by Austria-Hungary, Germany, and Russia. The outcome might have been different if Milan had explained his thinking to the people, if he had used the national militia as well as the standing army, if he had not dismissed most of the military commanders who led Serbia's forces against the Turks in 1876-1878, and if he had not held back certain forces which he wanted to have on hand in case of internal disorder.

The first consequence of the unsuccessful war was Milan's desire to abdicate, but his Progressive ministers dissuaded him in no uncertain terms. The realization that his estranged wife, Natalie, might assume the role of regent in the event of his abdication also deterred him. Moreover, Austria-Hungary wanted him to stay on the throne. Milan realized that in the then existing circumstances, if he stayed on the throne, he would somehow need to make peace with the Radicals. After an initial effort to promote a Progressive-Liberal agreement failed, Milan went to the Belgrade prison and enlisted the assistance of Pera Todorović, a member of the Radical Main Committee who was then serving a ten year sentence. Todorović was ready to do anything to get out of jail, but at a meeting of some 40 Radicals he was able to win over only one additional Radical in favor of a Progressive-Radical coalition.

Consequently, Milan had only one combination left, a Radical-Liberal agreement, which he succeeded in promoting after he pardoned the Radicals who were in prison as a result of the Timok Rebellion. New elections were held in April 1886, and the Radical-Liberal coalition would have won a majority if it had not been for open and brutal police pressure on the part of Progressive authorities.[10] The Progressives thereby managed to stay on, but only for a brief time. Their final downfall was closely associated with the estrangement of Milan and Natalie.

Milan and Natalie had separated before the Serb-Bulgarian war, in part because they were seemingly incompatible (among other things, Milan was not a faithful husband), and in part because she did not approve of Milan's pro-Austrian policy and his desire to educate their son, Alexander, in Vienna.[11] During the war she returned to Serbia and won considerable popularity through her concern for the wounded. Milan imagined that she wanted to drive him from the throne and that she wanted to become the regent, but it seems that she only gave thought to the latter after Milan had indicated that he wanted to abdicate for the whole dynasty. In any event, a mutual hatred for each other developed rapidly. Milan used a minor pretext— she had refused to extend her hand to a lady from the diplomatic corps whom she suspected (wrongly) of being Milan's mistress—to inform her by letter that life together for them was no longer possible and that she would have to leave Serbia.

Upon being informed of Milan's letter, his prime minister (Garašanin) resigned, but was persuaded to withdraw the resignation after an arrangement had been worked out for Natalie to live abroad. As a way of hiding their difficulties from the public, it was announced that Natalie would live abroad in connection with the education of their eleven-year old son. Nevertheless, Milan no longer had confidence in Garašanin, and was already plotting to make a change when word reached him, a piece of inaccurate news it seems, that Natalie was returning to Belgrade. He ordered that she be prevented from doing so by force if need be. The result was a stormy session between Milan and his prime minister, who resigned the following day.

Apparently, Milan had initially thought of separation, but his plans no doubt envisioned a possible divorce, as well as a new constitution that would empower him to appoint a regency during Alexander's minority. The man most likely to stand by him in his quarrel with Natalie, he believed, was a man he thoroughly disliked, Jovan Ristić. Since neither of the twin evils—living with Natalie or governing with Ristić—was acceptable to him, Milan decided that he should abdicate. But each step in that direction was fraught with difficulties and uncertainties.

His first step was to appoint a Liberal-Radical ministry in June, 1887, headed by Ristić. In the ensuing elections (September, 1887), the Liberals won only 59 seats and the Radicals 87, with the Progressives not participating. Soon Milan concluded that it would be easier to work with one party than with two. Since he believed that the Radicals were more amenable to his views on foreign policy, he let it be known that he would be willing to entrust his cabinet to them alone. Consequently, the coalition fell apart, and in December 1887, Colonel Sava Grujić was made prime minister. Although identified with the Radicals, Grujić had served as minister of war and had performed admirably in diplomatic assignments. Milan got a promise from Grujić that foreign policy would be left to him, and that there could be no amnesty for Nikola Pašić and the other Radicals. Nevertheless, on New Year's 1888, all Radicals except Pašić were pardoned, and Grujić was promoted to the rank of general.

In new elections, held in February 1888, the Radicals won all but 15 seats, which were held by Liberals, while the Progressives elected none. Milan was soon dissatisfied with the new Radical cabinet, mainly because Radical policies were not being decided by the cabinet but by the Radical caucus.[12] Grujić resigned in April 1888, after being in power less than four months, ostensibly because Milan refused to sign an act of the Skupština. The main reason behind Milan's distrust of Grujić, however, stemmed from the latter's apparent sympathy for Natalie, and his agreement with her position that Alexander should not be educated abroad. Milan erred in identifying Grujić's views with the Radical party, because it did not have a position on the question of Natalie, and Grujić was seemingly her only sympathizer in the party. As a consequence of his conviction, Milan believed that he needed another ministry to settle the problem.

Milan turned to the time-tested and dependable bureaucrat, Nikola Hristić, who in April 1888 put together a cabinet of civil servants and a few Progressives. Among them were known enemies of Natalie. Angered by a provocative letter from her, Milan submitted a petition for a divorce to the head of the Serbian Orthodox church and so informed her in Wiesbaden. In view of the fact that she held a precious hostage, Alexander, Milan became concerned lest she take off with him for Russia. He asked the German government to institute surveillance, but Chancellor Bismarck proposed a simpler solution. Milan should send a military officer to Wiesbaden and take Alexander away from Natalie. Milan sent the minister of war, General Kosta Protić, not to take the son away but to offer the queen a new agreement. Sensing that the king was afraid of a contested divorce, she refused. Thereupon Milan ordered Protić to take Alexander by force.

Protić needed the assistance of the German police, which asked Natalie to give up Alexander voluntarily. She requested three days to think it over, and then said she would surrender Alexander, not to General Protić, but to Milan directly. The Austrian cabinet, which had heretofore not been involved, advised Milan to go to Wiesbaden. At the last moment, the German minister advised Milan that it was too late, that the German police, on Bismarck's orders, had taken the matter into their own hands and had taken Alexander away from Natalie. Prior to the Wiesbaden incident Milan's and Natalie's troubles had been kept from public view. The forceful seizure of Alexander was characterized as scandalous, and Milan got most of the blame at home and abroad. Objectively speaking, Milan, Natalie, and Bismarck were all at fault.

Prior to Bismarck's act, Milan had offered Natalie a settlement which in many respects was generous. Preferring to avoid a public scandal, he proposed to drop the divorce action and to let her keep Alexander for five years, but she must stay away from Serbia. It was when she turned a deaf ear to these proposals that Milan ordered Protić to take direct action. After the Wiesbaden incident, Natalie became more yielding and Milan more uncompromising. Finally, he asked the Council of Bishops to act on his divorce petition, but the Council informed him that it lacked jurisdiction. Milan found this hard to take, for he had brought most of its members to their positions following the earlier ouster of Metropolitan Mihailo and many of his colleagues. As a last resort, he put pressure on Metropolitan Teodosije, who signed the divorce decree. No statute or legal decree was cited, only the passage from Matthew (ch. 16, verse 19): "...whatsoever thou shalt bind on earth shall be bound in heaven: and whatsoever thou shalt loose on earth shall be loosed in heaven."

The divorce decree, issued on October 12, 1888, placed Milan in an unfavorable light as far as the public was concerned. In the patriarchal Serbia of that day divorce, even when it involved ordinary citizens, was looked down upon, let alone when it concerned the monarch. In addition, the way in which Milan carried out the divorce was but new proof of his unbridled despotic disposition. Moreover, for several months, the business of government had given way to absorption in matters of his private life.

Victory for Parliamentary Government

Two days after the publication of his divorce decree, Milan ordered elections to take place on November 20, 1888 for the Large National Skupština, whose task would be to change the constitution.[13] Although constitutional reform had been under discussion for several years, Milan made the announcement without even having informed the prime minister of his intentions. On the day after he made the announcement, Milan appointed a committee of some eighty leading men from the three political parties to prepare a draft of a new constitution. He retained the presidency of the committee for himself, and made the leaders (Ristić, Garašanin, and Grujić) of the three respective parties as vice-presidents. The basic work of the committee was actually done by a sub-committee of 12, whose draft was in the main adopted by the full committee and by the constituent assembly.

Milan exercised a strong leading hand in all the deliberations. From the outset he made it clear that the new constitution had to be the common work of all parties. In essence it was the work of Milan, the Belgrade Radicals, and Jovan Ristić; the Progressives played a minor role. The king proved to be an effective presiding officer; he possessed that combination of patience and decisiveness which are sought in a good chairman. Moreover, he was able rather quickly to find the middle ground which the parties could accept, and sometimes he virtually forced them to do so. He was able to get the essence of a question after a quick briefing, and he was a gifted speaker. Finally, despite difficulties he was able to get agreement in the full committee (except for two Radicals) that all members would support the draft without amendments in the constituent assembly.

The Constitution of 1888 was a remarkably democratic document, one of the most liberal constitutions in Europe of that day. In essence it (1) explicitly established a parliamentary system, (2) strongly protected civil rights, and (3) recognized certain political powers for organs of local government. In several ways, the framers seem to have been influenced by the Belgian constitution.

In establishing a parliamentary system, the constitution retained the unicameral system, but it eliminated appointive deputies. All deputies were to be elected directly and by secret ballot. Proportional representation, although opposed by the Radicals, who feared that one party might not be able to get a majority in the Skupština under that system, was adopted because the Liberals and Progressives were adamant on the issue. Ministers could now be members of the Skupština, no longer looked upon as the king's servants but as men who came to their positions by virtue of the confidence of the Skupština. The powers of the latter were significantly widened in the legislative field as well as in being given control of finance. Milan was not happy with the explicit provision for a parliamentary system which denied to the monarch any real political power, but he went along.

In the area of civil rights the constitution was quite explicit, especially when it came to freedom of the press. It forbade censorship or any prior approval of what was to be printed. It also forbade administrative warnings, and generally followed the Belgian example with respect to responsibility for what was published. In another aspect of civil rights, the constitution guaranteed judicial independence and forbade the establishment of summary courts.

The Radicals, who had been the strongest advocates of local self-government and the most bitter critics of bureaucracy, did not get all they wanted in these areas. Nor did they eliminate the standing army. The increase in the powers of local government, especially when compared with the past, was a big step forward nonetheless.

As indicated above, ratification by the Large National Skupština was assured. It met on December 11, 1888 and formal approval came on December 22. Of around 600 members, the Radicals had about 500, the Liberals about 100, and the Progressives none. Milan told the Radicals clearly and openly that they could reject the draft—that was their right—but if they accepted it there could be no changes or additions. It had to be accepted "from cover to cover" or he would not sign it. In the end it was adopted, with some 75 Radicals voting against it.

Milan's approval of the Constitution of 1888 did not stem from a sudden conversion to democratic-parliamentary principles. On the contrary, he was planning to abdicate, and most of all, he wanted the power to appoint the regents during his son's minority, which the constitution gave him. Moreover, he was convinced that Serbia was not ready for such a constitution and that it would prove utterly unworkable. He was confident that within two years the ensuing chaos would lead the people, as well as the Great Powers, to beg him to return and to restore order. In this way, he would be rehabilitated and the Radicals would lose their support among the people. He may have been encouraged in this belief by virtue of the fact that his popularity, at a seemingly irretrievable low following his divorce, was in large measure restored by the adoption of the liberal-democratic constitution.

Milan's decision to abdicate was motivated by a number of factors. At different times he gave varied reasons: fear of insanity, marital troubles, disloyalty of Serbian politicians, and a desire to improve relations with Russia. In a letter to Kaiser Wilhelm II, Milan set the date of his abdication as February 22 (March 6), 1889, and alleged that the main reason for his abdication was his inability to agree with the new constitution.[14] In the same letter there is the following revealing paragraph:

> I cannot count on any political party, nor on any man here. It is impossible to rule forever with brutal power; and even the army carries out its duty as a duty, but not by conviction. During these twenty years I have had two revolutions to put down, to say nothing of greater or lesser conspiracies. Over time it becomes repulsive to shoot and imprison men. And every individual who comes out of prison becomes a popular political personality whom everyone likes and respects.

At the same time, note should be made of the fact that Milan had fallen in love with the wife (Artemiza) of his personal secretary, Milan Hristić, an affair he did not seek to hide. He fully expected her to get a divorce and marry him after his abdication. In a letter to her right after his abdication, he told her that the abdication was the greatest possible proof of his love.

Before abdicating Milan named a three-man regency. He chose Jovan Ristić as first regent even though he disliked him. The qualities that recommended Ristić were primarily two: he was a seasoned politician and no friend of the Radicals, and he had valuable experience, having headed the earlier regency during Milan's own minority. Moreover, he could be pressed, despite great reluctance, into giving Austria-Hungary the assurance that the secret treaty of 1881 would be adhered to. The other two regents were military men personally loyal to Milan, generals Kosta Protić and Jovan Belimarković.

The principal tasks of the regency, in Milan's view, were three. The first was to protect the dynasty from the Radicals by lulling them to sleep politically until the constitution proved unworkable. Secondly, he expected the regency to keep Natalie out of Serbia, particularly since none of the three members were friendly toward her. Thirdly, Ristić, as the one politician among them, would steer the nation's course politically, while Milan could continue to mix in Serbian affairs, through his two loyal military men, even after his abdication.

At age 35 Milan left the Serbian throne, parliamentarism triumphed, and the Radicals finally came to power. The Constitution of 1888 was the last act in the eight-year old struggle between the monarch and the Radical party. Ostensibly this was a victory for the latter. In fact it was only a partial and temporary victory, and Serbia was not to be free of Milan's intrigues until his death in 1901, some twelve years later. His abdication in 1889 was but the end of one chapter in a stormy political saga.

THE STRUGGLE CONTINUES, 1889-1903

The victory for parliamentary government symbolized by the Constitution of 1888 and King Milan's abdication in early 1889 was not to be consolidated until 1903. For several years the parliamentary system worked well, although the continuing quarrel between Milan and Natalie consumed an inordinate amount of time and energy of the political leaders. Just as this problem seemed to have been resolved, a Milan-Alexander duarchy came to dominate Serbian politics for several years. Then followed critical differences between father and son, the assertion of power by Alexander, his unpopular marriage, and the brutal end of the dynasty in 1903, together with the restoration of the Karadjordjević dynasty and of the 1888 constitution.

Government Under the Regency, 1889-1893

The Radicals formed the first cabinet under the regency and ushered in several years of stable parliamentary rule. The Radical leaders, most of them first-rate intellectuals (several were subsequently elected to the Academy of Sciences and Arts), demonstrated that they were responsible and able to perform the task of governing. More specifically, they proved (1) that a certain political stability was attainable, (2) that it was possible to govern constitutionally, and (3) that (1) and (2) could be achieved with the Radicals at the helm.

One of the first acts of the new cabinet was to pardon Nikola Pašić, an act recommended by none other than Milan, as a "friend" of the regency. Within a few months of his triumphal return, after the landslide victories of the Radicals in the elections of September 1889, Pašić was elected president of the Skupština. While everyone recognized that he was the real leader of the Radicals, it was considered prudent that he should not be made prime minister too soon after his return from exile. Two years later, in February 1891, he formed his first cabinet. Meanwhile, other Radical leaders were occupied with matters of more immediate concern.

Much legislation was needed to put the new constitution into force.[1] Among these acts were laws concerning the following: elections, freedom of the press, ministerial responsibility, the Council of State, meetings and organizations, local government, judiciary, the office of the comptroller, and the organization of the Army. In addition, the cabinet made peace with the Orthodox Church, and brought back Metropolitan Mihailo as head of the hierarchy.

Aside from enacting the necessary legislation to implement the new constitution, the Radicals moved quickly in passing certain economic and social measures.[2] One of their first acts was to nationalize the railroads, which was well-received at home but not abroad. The necessary agreements were nonetheless negotiated by October 1889, and the operation of the railroads by the government was successful. In addition, the cabinet moved to take over the salt and tobacco monopolies, which had also been controlled by foreigners. Moreover, a state lottery was instituted as a way of helping the economy, and concessions were provided as a way of encouraging domestic industry. All of these acts helped to reduce the financial deficits which the Radicals had inherited. Finally, other laws were passed to protect forests from vandalizing exploitation, to provide for "food banks" in the event of bad crop years, to establish trade and artisan schools, and to set up an institute to improve the breeds of all livestock.

In the foreign affairs field, the Radicals experienced tense relations with Austria-Hungary, and improved Serbian contacts with Russia. Relations with Bulgaria presented great difficulties for the Radicals, who realized how badly neglected were the Serbian areas still under Ottoman rule, especially the regions of the old Serbian empire (Macedonia and surrounding areas). In these regions, the Turks had forbidden Serbian schools, but had allowed the Bulgarians to move into Macedonia and to take over old Serbian churches and monasteries, as well as to open schools there. The Radicals worked more systematically on this problem than had other Serbian cabinets. Their efforts even convinced the Russians, who had supported a Great Bulgaria in the past, to wonder if perhaps they should not have two irons instead of one in the Balkan fire.

The Radicals had been in power scarcely more than a year when their major efforts were drained off to deal with problems concerning Milan and Natalie. Milan disliked the apparent smooth-functioning of the government under the new constitution. He came back to Serbia in May 1890, and because of the many rumors about his mixing in Serbian politics, the cabinet was compelled to issue official denials, i.e., that his activities were not impeding the normal functioning of the government. In August 1890 he wrote a letter to first regent Ristić, which was clearly anti-Radical. Soon thereafter he told Ristić orally: "Give me power, whether in one form or another, so that I can clean up this situation if you will not."[3] To this Ristić replied: "You know that I was the last to agree to your abdication. . . . If it comes to that that we have to give up power to some one prior to the constitutional term, then you will not be the one to whom we will give power but to the Large National Skupština. . . ."[4] Milan went away angry, but his anger did not nullify his ability to plot some more.

Natalie, for her part, turned to Metropolitan Mihailo, who had just been returned to his post, and asked that the earlier divorce decree, issued by his predecessor, be declared null and void. Without consulting the cabinet or the regency, Mihailo obliged. Thereupon Ristić had the unpleasant task of convincing him to issue a statement that the Church Council in full session had decided that it did not have the power to consider anew a matter that had already been decided. Natalie then addressed a memorandum to the Skupština, and the whole affair became a domestic political football, while the royal dirty linen received a washing in the foreign press. The Skupština found that it was not competent to deal with her memorandum. After months of delay and after the failure of the regents and the cabinet to pacify Natalie, the Radicals decided to sacrifice her, in part because they were more afraid of Milan. When she failed to leave Serbia, she was ordered to do so and a river boat was put at her disposal. She still refused and mobs of her sympathizers prevented the departure on the appointed day in May 1891. Early the next morning she was forcibly put on the train and was out of the country while the city still slept.

The forcible expulsion of Natalie was not a popular act. Earlier she had gained considerable sympathy because of the way Milan had divorced her. This sympathy grew by leaps and bounds when the Radical cabinet prevented her from going to the palace on her return to Serbia after Milan's abdication. Many Serbs pictured her as a pining mother, forced to live in a house in town, not being able to be with her son in the palace.

Even before Natalie was out of the way, Milan began to bargain with the Radicals. Bruised and annoyed by press stories of his gambling losses and other escapades, he wanted a change in the press law to protect him from such writing, and the Radicals grudgingly accommodated him. Moreover, for a lump sum settlement, instead of a monthly allowance from the civil list, he would leave Serbia until his son was of age. It was known that his debts in 1889 were sizable. In 1891, he asked for 6 million dinars, but settled for 1 million plus a promise from the government to find him a loan of 2 additional million to be secured by his real property in Serbia.[5] The loan was found in Russia, really a gift from the Russian tsar which was not public information at the time. In return Milan wrote a letter to the regency renouncing all his rights under the constitution, including citizenship and membership in the royal household, as well as the right to educate Alexander. The Skupština recognized Milan's action and thereby made the deal binding legally, an action that was made public in March 1892. The Skupština's act even stated that Milan could not become a Serbian citizen anew without its prior approval.

A few months later (June 1892), Regent Kosta Protić died suddenly, creating a crisis between the Radicals and the first regent, Ristić.[6] Under the constitution, the Skupština was empowered to fill such a vacancy, but it was not due to meet for several months. Prime Minister Pašić recommended a special session, but Ristić, suspecting that Pašić might be elected regent and thereby overshadow him, would not agree. Thereupon Pašić resigned, and Ristić asked a Liberal, Jovan Dj. Avakumović, to form a ministry, resulting in a bitter political struggle between the Liberals and the Radicals. In new elections, held in February 1893, the results were in some respects uncertain, although the Radicals clearly lost their majority. According to the calculations of the ministry of interior, the Liberals elected 70, the Radicals 50, and the Progressives 3, with some seats still to be decided. According to Radical calculations, however, the Liberals should get 66 seats, the Radicals 64, and the Progressives 4. In the end the Liberals were given 69 seats, a scant majority in a body of 134 deputies.

The April 1893 Coup: Alexander in Power, 1893-1897

The somewhat muddled parliamentary situation gave Milan a convenient opportunity to carry out his plans, which had been several months in the making, to engineer an overthrow of the regency.[7] The coup was bloodless. After a dinner at the palace, to which he invited the two regents and the ministers, Alexander arose as if to propose a toast. Instead, declaring himself of age (he was not yet 17), he told his honored guests that he had taken the royal powers into his own hands. While they had been dining, by prearranged plan, troops loyal to Alexander had seized the foreign and interior ministries, the city hall, and the telegraph. In addition, the homes of the ministers and the regents, as well as the Skupština building, had been surrounded. After his announcement, Alexander left the dining hall while

Ristić was beginning to reply. Subsequently, the regents were asked to resign, but they refused. Consequently, the king's guests became his prisoners for the night. The next morning found the city plastered with royal decrees, informing the public that Alexander had assumed power.

Milan's motives in engineering the coup were mixed. By 1892 he despaired of the new political system's collapsing. The differences that developed between the regency and the Radicals, following the death in the same year of Regent Protić, gave him some pretext to get involved. But these and other political reasons were no doubt secondary; his financial needs were uppermost in his motivation. Early in life he had acquired the habit of squandering money even when he did not have it. The money he had obtained in the lump sum settlement, worked out with the cabinet in 1891-1892, was gone by the autumn of 1892. In addition, he had pawned his furniture and silver, valued at 100,000 francs, as well as the jewels he had inherited from Prince Mihailo, which were worth between 300 and 400 thousand francs.[8]

In desperation, and completely sacrificing his self-respect, Milan turned to Natalie for help. In a long letter to her in January 1893, he informed her that he was going to commit suicide (but would try to make it seem as an accident), and asked that she give him 345,000 francs so as to pay off his debts and thus avoid leaving a legacy of embarrassment to their son.[9] He told her that he could get the money from Artemiza, but not under her conditions—marriage. He had planned to marry her after his abdication, but three years had dragged on before she had her divorce, and then Milan no longer wanted her even though she had a son by him. Natalie took him seriously enough to get together 100,000 francs—all that she could do—but on condition that he not commit suicide and that he redeem the family jewels and give them to Alexander.

Milan took the money, and faithful to his habits, soon spent it. With Artemiza's help he got a loan from the Sultan of 500,000 francs, paid his debts, but was soon broke again.[10] He quickly realized that his financial woes could be cured only if he could get his hands on some of the unspent money in the civil list. But there were guardians of this money in the palace, and the only way he could get it was through a coup. Apparently acting on the assumption that the coup would be more palatable if the reputation of the dynasty could be improved, Milan spread a rumor that there had been a reconciliation with Natalie. He even went so far as to ask the

Orthodox Church Council to proclaim the earlier divorce decree null and void, and the Council fulfilled his request in February 1893.[11]

Indeed, the coup was not too unpopular, especially among the Radicals, who were still smarting from Ristić's preventing them from electing a regent the previous year. The first prime minister after the coup was Dr. Lazar Dokić, a professor of anatomy, a one-time tutor of Alexander's, and president of the Council of State. A moderate Radical by conviction although not a party member, he managed to get the cooperation of many Radicals, but not that of the party leader, Pašić, who was sent to Petrograd as Serbia's minister as a way of getting him out of the way. Dokić's cabinet immediately dissolved the Liberal-controlled Skupština, and at new elections in May the Radicals received over 88 per cent of the votes cast, and won all but some ten seats.

Relations between the young monarch and the Radicals soon began to sour. When because of Dokić's illness it was necessary to form a new cabinet, Alexander and the Radical caucus differed sharply. Earlier Alexander had met in Abacija with his father, who did not yet dare to come to Serbia, but who was free with advice. Consequently, Sava Grujić, a moderate Radical who had served under Milan, was appointed prime minister, but his cabinet resigned in January 1895 when Alexander faced them with a *fait accompli*— he had invited his father to come to Serbia and indeed he was already on the way.

After Milan's return, Alexander sought to rule through several relatively neutral cabinets. In May 1894, when the Court of Cassation threw out a decree that would have nullified the law which forbade his father's return, Alexander abolished the Constitution of 1888 and returned to the more conservative one of 1869, thus pulling off a coup with a stroke of the pen. This was a hard blow to the Radicals, because to them the Constitution of 1888 symbolized all that they had fought for politically,[12] and because after this second coup there was a systematic cleaning out of Radicals from the civil service.

The young monarch found himself in the middle—he was getting contradictory advice from his father and his mother. Milan advised governing with any combination except the Radicals, while Natalie argued that the only way to safeguard the dynasty was to work with the Radicals and in any case not against them. Initially, Alexander leaned towards his father's views, but for about two and a half years (1895-1897), he seemed to be under the influence of his mother.

For one thing, by contrast with Milan, she did not want anything for herself. More important, but unknown to Natalie, was her lady-in-waiting, the widow Draga Mašin. Although twelve years older than Alexander, Draga had caught his eye during visits to his mother and he had fallen in love with her.

Nevertheless Alexander still distrusted the Radicals, partly because they always seemed to be talking about constitutional reform. One of their most gifted polemicists, Stojan Protić, who had been influenced by the writings of the Englishman, Walter Bagehot, had argued in Radical publications that parliamentary government had to be party government, and that the crown should be above political struggles. In view of his distrust of the Radicals, Alexander for a time managed with several ministerial combinations in which the Radicals were usually present but whose voice was not dominant. Natalie had only half convinced him that he needed to make peace with the Radicals.

In December 1896, however, he entrusted the formation of the cabinet to Djordje Simić, a moderate Radical who a brief time earlier had presided over a politically neutral cabinet. While the second Simić cabinet also contained a number of nonpolitical personalities, the Radicals were dominant. Simić was in effect an intermediary between the king and the Radicals. Before his appointment of Simić, Alexander had sought and received a promise from the party leader, Pašić, that the constitutional issue would be postponed for a time, ostensibly because of foreign policy problems.

The life of the Simić cabinet was short. It nearly collapsed when Alexander invited his father to come to Belgrade during the Christmas holidays. In June 1897, new elections were held in which the Progressives and Liberals did not take part, with the result that the Radicals won every seat. Because the Constitution of 1869 was then in force, the king appointed 25 Radicals, 15 Liberals, 7 Progressives, and 12 nonparty deputies. Later in the summer, after a visit abroad with his father and mother, Alexander made a final break with his mother, probably because she was pushing him to marry a European princess, although presumably not knowing of his love for Draga. In October, he came back to Belgrade with his father, and immediately dismissed the Simić cabinet. This ended the first phase of Alexander's rule after the coup of April 1893, a brief period that witnessed seven separate ministries.[13]

The Milan-Alexander Duarchy, 1897-1900

By contrast with the previous period, the time of the duarchy had only one cabinet, that of Dr. Vladan Djordjević, a renowned surgeon. None of his proposed cabinet appointments, however, was acceptable to the kings. Presiding over a cabinet he did not appoint, he merely acted out the role of prime minister. He and the ministers were not initiators of policies—this was performed by the kings. As a matter of fact, Alexander did not tolerate ministerial sessions without his presence. If he found two ministers talking, he immediately demanded to know what they had been talking about.

The political system during the Djordjević cabinet can best be characterized as a nonparty personal regime, firm and strict. It was based on the proposition that party struggles had been bad for Serbia. Consequently, the government ruled without opposition, and with increasing arrogance. Radicals were purged from the civil service. The press was effectively muzzled, and members of the Skupština— chosen by the police instead of the people—did not feel secure and did not dare to take issue with positions taken by the ministers or the monarch. The Radicals, who had announced that they would constitute themselves as a loyal opposition, were frustrated at every turn. Their leader, Pašić, went to jail for nine months in 1898, because of a piece in a party publication wherein he admitted that he had opposed Milan.[14] The only opposition that made itself felt came in the way of underground pamphlets and leaflets from abroad, no doubt the work of Radicals.

A few months after taking office, the Djordjević cabinet held elections in May 1898. The candidates were handpicked from persons known to be loyal to the crown. The results were as follows: Liberals 112; Progressives 62; Radicals 1; nonparty 19. Although carefully chosen, the Liberal deputies were still a concern to Alexander and Milan as long as Ristić was head of the Liberal Main Committee. Considerable pressure was exerted on him to give up his post, and when he failed to do so, his son was demoted from secretary in the Serbian legation in Paris to the position of postman.[15] When this failed to move Ristić, the government put a stop to the publication of the Liberal party organ. Alexander's and Milan's worries were seemingly groundless, because the Skupština caused them no headaches.

Nevertheless, the kings were taking no chances in their determination to strengthen the dynasty. From the outset King Father Milan was named commandant of the army, a position he held for two and a half years, until an irreparable break with his son. The latter, for his part, introduced medals, autographed portraits, and other ways of buying support, while force as a royal weapon was not relinquished. When one of his ministers suggested that there might be need to let up a little, referring to the role of the English queen, Alexander retorted: "Why are you mentioning that English queen who stands so high that she cannot be seen or her presence felt! There is nothing to that."[16]

As commandant of the army, Milan became a type of state within a state. He saw to it that large sums were spent on building up the army, and yet not even cabinet ministers dared to discuss the army budget or other military matters. Milan took his duties seriously, and was popular with the officers. He was the first civilian chief of the armed forces. He did not have military training nor was he a military expert. Perhaps for these reasons, he did not get bogged down in details or formalities, but quickly grasped the main needs and subordinated everything else to them. The army was an expensive item, and mainly because of it the Djordjević cabinet experienced constant budgetary deficits.

The politically neutral Skupština passed a large number of constructive laws, but it also severely limited the press and it in effect abolished political parties.[17] Alexander at one point said that if he had his way he would introduce whippings for newsmen.[18] The regime also introduced reforms in the school system and in the bureaucracy, with the aim of preventing penetration by allegedly subversive elements. Usually, the special target was the Radical party and its friends.

In foreign affairs, the cabinet and the two kings were caught in a diplomatic crossfire between Austria-Hungary and Russia.[19] The two powers had reached an agreement in 1897 to respect the status quo in the Balkans, but both were trying to undermine each other's influence in Sofia and Belgrade. One of Alexander's main efforts was to repair relations between the Russians and his father, but this was to no avail. Relations with Vienna continued to be excellent during the Djordjević ministry. The former put no obstacles in the way of Serbia's export of livestock, which had not been true during some earlier Serbian cabinets. Djordjević reciprocated by not permitting the Serbian press to criticize Austria-Hungary or to speak of the need to unite Serbian lands.

Toward the end of the Djordjević regime, two major events shook Serbia, and to a degree Europe as well. The first was the attempt on Milan's life in June 1899, for which the Radicals were blamed and as a result of which at least two of their leaders escaped death sentences through foreign intervention. The second, a year later, was Alexander's decision to marry Draga Mašin, causing a final break with his father, who left Serbia never to return.

There is still a great deal of dispute as to the attempt on Milan's life, with some allegations that the whole affair was staged so as to provide the government with a pretext to act against the Radicals.[20] In any event, the very evening it happened an order went out from the palace to arrest Pašić, who had just returned from a nine-month prison sentence, and other Radical leaders. The next day a massive persecution of Radicals began, and a summary court was created to try those allegedly involved in the assassination attempt. The latter news was ill-received at home and abroad. Interestingly enough, at this very time the Dreyfus case had been re-opened in France because of the widespread belief that an innocent man had been convicted, and all of Europe was talking about it. Nevertheless, Milan was insistent that at least Pašić and Kosta Taušanović, another member of the Radical Main Committee, must be sentenced to death.

Fortunately for them, Russia and Austria-Hungary, for different reasons, stepped in to save them. Russia because if they were put to death, no Serbian party could ever be pro-Russian, and Austria-Hungary because she feared that Russia would act in that eventuality, which would destroy their agreement of 1897 to maintain the status quo in the Balkans. The mouth organ of the Vienna cabinet, *Der Fremdenblatt*, wrote, even before the trial, that the guilt of the Radicals had not been established. And while the trial was in progress, Vienna sent her military attaché to inform Milan and Alexander that they could not execute Pašić and Taušanović, else the dynasty would be boycotted by all of Europe.

Finding himself in a position not too much unlike that after the Timok Rebellion and the war with Bulgaria, Milan sent the minister of interior, Djordje Genčić, to the Belgrade prison in an effort to make a deal with Pašić. In return for an admission that he had tolerated anti-dynastic elements in the party, Pašić could save his life and those of other Radicals. Otherwise up to twelve heads would roll. Not knowing that his life had already been saved by foreign intervention, Pašić agreed. This was perhaps the toughest moment in his life, for it seemed that he was a man without an ounce of courage, and yet it could not be publicly revealed that the king's emissary had come to the prison to seek the deal. As a consequence, Pašić became the most unpopular man in the country, a factor which triggered a split in the Radical party.[21]

The summary court sentenced two men to death, the would-be assassin and an associate who had fled the country. It also convicted some 15 Radical leaders, with most of them getting twenty-year prison terms. Pašić and Taušanović were tried separately, with Pašić getting five years and Taušanović eight. Pašić was immediately pardoned, and Taušanović's sentence reduced to three years. The only proof against any of the Radical leaders was that they had made anti-dynastic statements or had been responsible for the circulation of underground literature that contained bitter and vicious attacks on Milan.

The other event that shook Serbia in the last year of the Djordjević cabinet was Alexander's decision to marry Draga, a widow ten years his senior.[22] When informed of his desire, the cabinet resigned, but the king would not accept the resignation until the engagement was formally announced. This was in July 1900. Earlier in the year, the young king had told his father that he would marry a certain German princess. When new of the "bolt out of the blue" reached him, Milan, who was abroad at the time, resigned his position as commandant of the army. Natalie was also opposed to the marriage. Milan, in a letter to his son, as a parting shot, wrote: "If this decision of yours is irrevocable, as you say, then there is nothing left for me but to pray for the fatherland. After this impulsive act, I would be the first to greet the government which would overthrow you."[23]

Alexander's decision was not generally popular, and had Milan given the word the army would probably have dethroned him. Alexander must have had some fears of this, because he ordered that his father be stopped by force, if necessary, if he attempted to return. At the same time Alexander soon realized how unpopular the proposed marriage was, because he was unable to get any known politician to head a "wedding ministry." Even the "old reliable," Nikola Hristić, changed his mind overnight, after having agreed to take on the task. Moreover, no general could be found to accept the post of minister of war. Finally, a lieutenant colonel was put in the post. Aware of the unpopularity of his decision, Alexander nodded slightly toward the Radicals. On the same day that he announced the "wedding ministry," he pardoned the Radicals who had been convicted of the attempt to assassinate his father a year earlier.

After the marriage, which took place a few days following the announcement, and after the initial shock and disbelief had passed, public opinion began to change. More and more people began to say that a native wife was better than a German princess. This opinion was no doubt reinforced by the news that the Russian tsar had agreed to become the godfather, and the realization that Milan's influence in Serbia was finally at an end. Ironically, Milan died some six months later in Vienna, a grieving and dejected "old man" who had not yet reached his 47th birthday.

The Last Days of Alexander's Reign

Milan's death in January 1901 lifted the burden of fear from the royal couple. During the previous several months Milan's friends and Draga's enemies were purged from government service, especially from the army, and Milan himself had been under constant surveillance. With the fear of Milan removed, Alexander faced other problems. The Radicals became bolder and began to raise the constitutional question. Alexander had known that he could not govern indefinitely with the "wedding ministry"; he had planned elections, but elections in which he could determine how many deputies each party would have. Milan's death spoiled these plans. One burden replaced another.

Alexander was successful, however, in promoting a Radical-Progressive agreement, which led to a new constitution. The Radical-Progressive cabinet was formed in March under the leadership of a Radical, Mihailo Vujić, and the new constitution octroyed by Alexander in April 1901.[24] The new constitution brought some liberalization, but as a half-measure it whetted the appetite for political freedoms but did not satiate them. Hoping to bridle the Radicals, Alexander created an upper house, the Senate, most of whose members he appointed. While paying lip-service to certain democratic postulates, the constitution passed over in silence such questions as the political responsibility of ministers.

The Radical-Progressive agreement was short-lived. The Radicals, who viewed the new constitution as the best they could get under the circumstances, nevertheless did well at the new elections held in July 1901. Five groups or parties entered the electoral contests, but the Radicals won 84 seats out of a total of 130 in the Skupština. In the Senate they won 17 of 18 elective senators, but after Alexander's appointments they had a total of 28 out of 58, less than a majority.[25] Despite their strength, the Radicals were allowed only three cabinet posts while the Progressives had four. After several cabinet crises, a new ministry was appointed in October 1902 under the leadership of one of the older Radical leaders, Pera Velimirović, but this was a poorer edition of the Vujić cabinet. It fell within a month, which ended the Radical-Progressive agreement, and Alexander returned to a personal regime.

One consequence of the Radical-Progressive agreement was to augment the division within Radical ranks. Already alienated to a degree because of Pašić's "cowardly" behavior before the summary court in 1899, the younger Radicals, in the main lawyers and professors, criticized the agreement as a retreat from the Radical party program. They viewed the 1901 constitution, not as a political necessity, but as a betrayal of the Constitution of 1888, and as an opportunism of fear. Although not desiring a final split in the party, the dissident Radicals did enter the 1901 elections as a separate group, as Independent Radicals, and managed to elect 14 deputies, while the pro-agreement Radicals elected 84. But the Independent Radicals were here to stay as a separate political party.

Alexander's return to personal rule did not solve his problems. A month after his marriage it was announced that the queen was pregnant, and when this turned out to be false, and a deliberate ruse, the public was not amused. Nor were people pleased by Draga's apparent domination over the young monarch. Not only was her birthday celebrated in grand style, but her name was given to army regiments, schools, and peasant villages. Alexander does not seem to have realized that the marriage, and subsequent events associated with it, were morally impermissible and politically impossible.

Stung by things appearing in the press, Alexander in March 1903 suspended the constitution for forty-five minutes in the middle of the night. During that brief period several laws that permitted a relatively free press and other political activities were repealed or amended, and the more stringent laws from an earlier period were re-enacted. The new elections held in early May were boycotted by most political groups and no opposition deputies were elected.

Meanwhile, dissatisfaction with Alexander's regime had been growing. This was especially true of the army, where even young officers had come to believe that Alexander's marriage to Draga, whom they regarded as a woman with a promiscuous past, had brought dishonor to the whole officer corps. Moreover, demoralization among the officers was aggravated by the fact that after Milan's departure material conditions in the army deteriorated sharply. In addition, salary payments were several months in arrears. Finally, the opposition press had tended to incite the officers.

In late May 1903, a conspiracy that had been in the making for two years resulted in the assassination of Alexander and Draga.[26] Initially, the conspiracy was the work of young officers, who constantly widened their circle. Since they did not have any special political orientation, they involved a small group of civilians, but no known Radicals or Karadjordjević followers. The officers viewed their task as getting rid of the king and queen. The task of the civilians was to choose a new king and a new prime minister. Alexander did not understand the nature or strength of officer dissatisfaction. He viewed news of a possible conspiracy as an effort to create a quarrel between him and the army. In addition to Alexander and Draga, the conspirators also killed the prime minister and the minister of war, while the minister of interior was seriously wounded. There was no plan to kill any ministers; this was decided upon hastily after the palace had been entered and when for a time Alexander and Draga were nowhere to be found. The death of the royal couple marked the extinction of the Obrenović dynasty and the end of a twenty-year struggle between this dynasty and the Radical party.

PART III
PARLIAMENTARY GOVERNMENT IN OPERATION

IX. SERBIA UNDER PARLIAMENTARY RULE
1903-1918

The year 1903 opened an extraordinary decade for Serbia. It was a decade of democratic rule, characterized by economic growth and a renaissance in the fields of education, literature, and the arts. It was a time, also, of domestic and foreign troubles. Nevertheless, it was a period of great achievements at home and abroad—a period of balanced budgets, and considerable territorial gains from the decaying Ottoman empire, as a result of the Balkan wars. It was a decade, too, when the Austro-Hungarian empire sought to prevent the Serbs from realizing their goals, finally declaring war on them in 1914. The end of the war in 1918 found the Serbs uniting with their brethren in Montenegro, Bosnia-Hercegovina, Vojvodina, and with other South Slavs to form the Kingdom of the Serbs, Croats, and Slovenes, later known as Yugoslavia.

Return of Parliamentary Rule

The conspirators who ended the Obrenović dynasty turned power over to an all-party coalition, which legitimized the return of parliamentary rule by calling into session the parliament that had been chosen under the Constitution of 1901. The parliament merely ratified previously agreed-upon acts—mainly the choice of Peter Karadjordjević as king and the return of the democratic Constitution of 1888, now to be known as the Constitution of 1903. With these changes Serbia again became a constitutional parliamentary monarchy.

The new king was the grandson of Karadjordje, the leader of the first Serbian revolt against the Turks in 1804. Aside from the Karadjordjević name, Peter had a number of qualities that endeared him to his fellow Serbs. He had translated John Stuart Mill's essay *On Liberty* into Serbian, prefaced with an introduction permeated with the spirit of democracy. This was circulated widely, though surreptitiously, in Serbia. In the Franco-Prussian war of 1870 he had fought in the French army and was wounded. In 1876 he had fought, under an assumed name, in the Serbian uprising against the Turks in Bosnia-Hercegovina, a popular and courageous act. As king, he not only became a constitutional monarch, but in addition, he earned the love and respect of the people by his modest and frugal way of life, so becoming a true son of a people who still had a long way to go in economic development.

Although the Constitution of 1903 restored a free and vigorous political life, Serbia's new leaders were determined to strengthen the nation's constitutional order through important reforms. The constitution was amended so as to give the cabinet control over finance, making it impossible for the Skupština to engage in irresponsible financial acts. In addition, a Court of Accounts, whose members were chosen for life by the Skupština, was established as a type of comptroller, serving as an independent check on the validity of government expenditures. Moreover, to secure the rule of law, the independence of the judiciary was secured by making judges irremovable. Finally, a system of administrative courts was created, with the Council of State as the supreme administrative tribunal, as an easy and inexpensive way that citizens could challenge acts of government officials which they believed to be contrary to the law.

Political decision-making was left to the people's representatives in the Skupština. These were chosen in hotly contested elections, mainly between the Radicals and the Independent Radicals (or just Independents). The other political parties that had played a role in the latter part of the nineteenth century—the Liberals and the Progressives—had spent themselves in power and had finished their historical mission with the end of the Obrenović era.

The Radicals, for whom the masses voted overwhelmingly in every free election, developed an internal split at the turn of the century. The rift stemmed in large measure from the dissatisfaction of vigorous intellectuals with the party's leadership, principally Nikola Pašić, the party leader. They were horrified with what they regarded as Pašić's cowardice before the summary court in 1899, when his life was at stake. This feeling was widely shared throughout party ranks, and it gave the intellectuals hope that they would inherit the leadership. Many of the Independents insisted that Pašić was not sufficiently energetic, and some of them even looked down upon his peasant background. Moreover, the Independents were encouraged by the widespread popularity they enjoyed as a result of their courageous opposition during the last years of Alexander's reign. When they saw that Pašić was beginning to rehabilitate himself, however, and was continuing his compromising position through support of the Obrenović Constitution of 1901, most of them realized that they were on the way to forming a new political party. But in the years after 1903, while always a serious challenge to the Radicals, the Independents had little success at the polls.

The first elections under the new constitution, held in September 1903, did not give any party a majority. Consequently, a coalition of Radicals and Independents formed a cabinet, under the leadership of Sava Grujić, a moderate and conciliatory Radical. The cabinet stayed in power for a little over a year, being replaced in November 1903 with a Radical cabinet under the party's leader, Nikola Pašić. The coalition cabinet had been unable to resolve basic disagreements over finance, building of new railroads, rearmament, and relations with the military.[1] Pašić succeeded in obtaining a slender majority for his cabinet by getting the leader of the Independents, Ljuba Živković, and a few of his friends to return to the Radical fold. The Independents, many of whom even up to that time may have nurtured hopes of becoming the dominant force in the Radical party, responded by electing a new leader, Ljuba Stojanović, and launched themselves as a fully separate and independent party.

Confronted by parliamentary obstructionist tactics on the part of the Independents, Pašić resolved to improve upon his slender majority through new elections. King Peter, however, refused his request for a dissolution and new elections, possibly the one unparliamentary act of his reign. Pašić resigned. The king then proceeded to appoint Stojanović prime minister, and almost immediately to grant his request for a dissolution. This act on the part of the monarch—to refuse Pašić's request and then to grant it to his successor—seemed contrary to traditional parliamentary practice, and was publicly criticized in the Radical press. After a hard-fought campaign, the Independents won 81 out of 160 parliamentary seats, the slenderest possible majority.

The Stojanović cabinet was in power for less than a year. Its prestige and authority were undermined by its attempt to conclude a loan with a Viennese bank and to negotiate an arms purchase agreement with Austro-Hungarian firms. In view of Serbia's past difficulties with Austria-Hungary, these plans received a hostile public reception. When the Skupština refused to approve the loan agreement, the Stojanović cabinet resigned. The king turned to the Radicals, who in new elections in April 1906 won a solid majority. The Independents never recovered. From that time until the formation of Yugoslavia in December 1918, the Radicals were in power, with Pašić as prime minister most of the time. For tactical reasons, however, he gave up the premiership briefly on certain occasions, usually to another Radical. And after Austria-Hungary's declaration of war on Serbia in

1914, an all-party coalition cabinet under Pašić was formed, but the coalition came apart in 1917, of which more will be said subsequently.

Domestic Political Struggles

In the course of the decade prior to World War I, Serbia's relatively new and hard-won democratic political system was confronted with a number of thorny domestic problems. These had to be handled in the context of a great deal of inexperience, and even intolerance, among the politicians, to say nothing of the slender Radical majorities. And they had to be considered along with ambitious programs in the social, economic, and cultural fields. Moreover, the thorny domestic questions were not unrelated to difficulties in the foreign realm, described in the subsequent section.

Perhaps the most critical domestic questions were: (1) the sensitive matter of the conspirators who overthrew the Obrenović dynasty, (2) the need for foreign loans, mainly for rearmament, (3) the abdication of Prince George, the heir to the throne, and (4) the problem of civil-military relations. The first two were of immediate concern, the third was not long in coming, and the fourth evolved more or less gradually. The Pašić cabinet succeeded in finding solutions to the first three, but the fourth continued to plague the king and the cabinet into the World War I years, and led finally to the trial and conviction of several army officers in 1917. These will be treated briefly in turn.

Much of Europe was horrified by the brutal assassination of the Obrenovićes, and the new Serbian king was publicly attacked in some foreign newspapers for surrounding himself with murderers. Great Britain broke diplomatic relations with Serbia, and demands were heard in many foreign circles for punishment of the conspirators. King Peter was uneasy, for the conspirators had brought him to the throne. And the conspirators added to the difficulties. Instead of abiding by their oath that if the conspiracy succeeded they would not seek personal rewards for themselves, they (about 60 in number) sought to make themselves bosses of the army and to be influential at the palace. In that way they created a gulf between themselves and the experienced politicians in the parliamentary regime.

Since in Serbia punishment could not even be mentioned, seemingly the only way out was to pension the conspirators, a solution acceptable to the British and certain other foreign circles. King Peter was at first opposed, believing that this was a drastic solution to a delicate matter. He preferred a voluntary agreement by which the conspirators would step down, but they were not cooperative. Prime Minister Pašić, however, was unwavering, cool, and logical. Through long and patient talks, he got the older conspirators to retire by giving them full pay, and King Peter approved.[2] Although this was not strictly legal, it was a way of resolving a delicate question without quarrels and without scandal. The younger officers, who at that time were not involved in politics, were allowed to remain on active service, with the understanding that they would not get involved in politics. The fact that they failed to abide by this understanding was to continue as a source of latent conflict between the civil and the military authority.

The question of Serbia's rearmament was critical on two counts: (1) the Radical cabinet was determined that the state budget should be balanced (and was), which meant that foreign loans were needed if the army was to be modernized, and (2) Austria-Hungary wanted to be the lender, as a way of making Serbia dependent on Vienna both politically and economically. As pointed out above, the Independents had negotiated a loan and an arms purchase agreement with Vienna but this was rejected by the Skupština. Pašić's Radical cabinet was convinced that Serbia must seek to liberate herself from dependence on Vienna. At the same time, Pašić knew that it would be suicidal for Serbia to get involved militarily with Austria, particularly at a time when Russia could not be relied upon for help so soon after her defeat by Japan.

The Austro-Hungarian leaders were convinced that Serbia had no choice, because they could interrupt Serbia's foreign trade, most of which was with the dual monarchy. This position was also shared by Serbian economic experts. Pašić, for his part, gave oral promises that he was willing to conclude agreements with Vienna, but delayed matters until opposition to such agreements could increase in the Skupština. When Austria demanded that the question be resolved, Pašić indicated his willingness but pointed out that the Skupština was opposed. Thereupon the Austrian leaders lost their patience and closed her borders to Serbia's trade. By his tactics, Pašić had risked a tariff war, and now he was in it, but he did not waver. His response was to conclude a loan in France and to purchase cannons for the Serbian army from French firms. Although the tariff war was to last for several years (to be discussed below), and to cause Serbia serious economic difficulties, the decisiveness of Pašić's cabinet promoted Serbia's political and economic independence.

The abdication in March 1909 of Prince George, the heir to the throne, came about as a result of several factors. The immediate cause was the death of his orderly, whom George had kicked in the stomach because he suspected that the orderly was an instrument of his enemies. More important were his anti-parliamentary statements, and especially his enmity toward the Radical leader, Pašić. Also contributing to his abdication, especially the timing, were his war-like statements to the foreign and domestic press at the time of the Bosnia-Hercegovina annexation crisis (1908-1909). While George says that he abdicated voluntarily, he was really forced to renounce all rights and prerogatives which the constitution had accorded him.[3] A number of his antics in his personal life probably also contributed to the conclusion of Serbia's political leaders that he was not fit to be king.[4]

It cannot be said that George did not know what he was doing. He admits that his father and others told him what his proper role should be in a constitutional monarchy.[5] Among other things, his father told him that "a king does not dare to disagree with his ministers. For him they represent the people, and the people's will is law." Moreover, while George was in school in Russia, he says that some influential Russian princes had told him that his views should be in conformity with those of Pašić, because cabinets having a parliamentary majority decided policy independently of the crown.

These admonitions had little impact on George. He admits that he told his father openly that he would never collaborate with Pašić. This haughty attitude toward the essence of a parliamentary system was compounded by his unconstitutional attempt to communicate directly with the Skupština. He regarded Pašić as his principal opponent, but admits that he undestimated Pašić's patience and determination.[6] Even after his abdication, George could not refrain from criticizing Pašić, at least to his father and to his brother Alexander, who was the new heir to the throne. The fact that his father told him that one day Alexander would be king and would have to work with Pašić, because as the leader of the largest political party "the constitution gives him the right to direct the country's politics," does not seem to have impressed George.

The question of the relationship of the civil and the military authority had its inception in the pensioning of the officer-conspirators in 1906, discussed above.[7] The hostility toward Pašić and the Radicals that it produced in Army ranks might have faded with the years if it had not been for Austria-Hungary's increasing threat to Serbia's national security. This threat was made evident by Vienna's tariff war and by her annexation of the largely Serbian lands of Bosnia-Hercegovina, as well as by the hostility toward Serbia found in the

Austro-Hungarian press. One reaction to this threat was the creation in Serbia of patriotic societies with an increasing affinity for the military. One of these, the Union or Death group (sometimes referred to as the "Black Hand"), was a secret revolutionary organization whose primary base was among officers in the army.[8] The aim of the organization was to work toward the union of all Serbian lands by whatever means. In setting this task for the organization, its leaders were in effect taking unto themselves an attribute of state power, contrary to the basic principles of a constitutional state and in fundamental conflict with military laws.

For some time, the conflict between the civil and the military authority was subdued, and during the Balkan wars (1912-1913) it was scarcely evident. Soon after these wars, during which many of the pensioned officer-conspirators were returned to active service, the conflict was brought out into the open in veiled exchanges between the official publications of Union or Death and the Radical party.[9] The bone of contention was the Pašić cabinet's desire to place the newly-liberated territories under civilian rule at an early date, the wisdom of which was questioned in some army circles. After a number of conflicts in these areas between civil and military personnel, the Pašić cabinet issued an official order that the civil authority had priority. The commandant at Skoplje, General Damjan Popović, refused to abide by this order and was promptly dismissed.[10] The moving force in Union or Death, Colonel Dragutin Dimitrijević-Apis, even suggested to some of his military colleagues that it would be a good thing if some of the civil administrators were forced to leave for home with all of their baggage.[11] And the official Union or Death publication attacked the minister of war for turning over the officer corps to the mercies of the Radicals.[12]

The response of the Pašić cabinet was to retire or transfer many of the officer-conspirators, but the situation had become complicated by the fact that some of the Independents had joined the fray in the desire to exploit the conflict for their political advantage. Articles criticizing the cabinet, written by Pašić's opponents, appeared in the Union or Death publication. King Peter, who may have been inclined toward the Independents, asked Pašić to change certain provisions in the cabinet decree concerning the priority of the civil authority, but the cabinet stood firm.[13] Pašić, believing that it was desirable to put the issue to the voters, especially since he had a majority of only seven votes in the Skupština, submitted his resignation and asked for a dissolution and new elections.

Many expected the monarch to turn to the Independents, but he was only willing to do so if they could agree on a coalition cabinet, which proved impossible. The king was motivated in large part by the fact that the Russian minister in Belgrade, Nikola Hartwig, had informed him that Russia had confidence only in Pašić.[14] Moreover, he was told by the French minister, apparently on Russia's urgings, that a new cabinet could not count on French financial assistance in the same measure as Pašić's cabinet.[15] Thereupon, the king granted Pašić's request, and almost immediately transferred the royal powers to his son Alexander. His inability or unwillingness to deal decisively with the civil-military conflict was certainly one of the principal reasons for this act.

Serbia's outstanding military victories against the Austro-Hungarian forces in the first year of the war resulted in a great deal of domestic tranquility. Her defeats in the fall of 1915 and the terrible and costly withdrawal through the Albanian mountains in winter, however, rekindled the conflict. Many officers believed that the tragedy could have been averted if Pašić had permitted them to attack the Bulgarian forces and thus to move toward Salonika. But since the Allies were still hoping to win Bulgaria over to their side, Pašić had not wanted to incur Russia's wrath by such an act. In exile on the Greek island of Corfu, Colonel Apis and his collaborators made no secret of their hostility toward Pašić and the Radicals. One of them even suggested that the latter would ultimately have to return to the homeland through "the gate of swords."[16] The challenge to the civil authority was clear.

When Serbian forces were on their way back to Serbia, Colonel Apis and some twenty of his collaborators were arrested in December 1916 and tried before a military court in June 1917 and convicted.[17] Nine were sentenced to be shot, three of whom were actually executed, among them Apis. The main charge against the group was that they had been responsible for an attempt on Alexander's life and of conspiring to overthrow the duly constituted government. Whatever one thinks of the evidence presented, the appropriateness of the penalties, or the motives of the principals on both sides, it is clear that Alexander and Pašić—who had no love for each other—were in agreement that some settling of accounts between the civil and the military authorities could not be avoided or long delayed. And whatever one thinks of their judgment, there seems little doubt that Apis and his collaborators exceeded the proper role of the military in a democratic political system.

Foreign Affairs Problems

In the decade prior to World War I, Serbia's foreign affairs difficulties were almost exclusively with Austria-Hungary.[18] The leaders in Vienna believed that a truly independent Serbia would be a threat to the dual monarchy, because Serbia would gain strength as she annexed Serbian areas of the decaying Ottoman empire, and a strong Serbia would constitute a powerful attraction to the South Slav inhabitants in Austria-Hungary. The Viennese rulers concluded, therefore, that Serbia should be prevented from annexing areas under Turkish rule, that she must not be allowed to join hands with the other Serbian state, Montenegro, and that she must not be permitted access to the Adriatic sea.

To achieve these objectives, and correspondingly to strengthen her position in the Balkans, Austria-Hungary undertook three major actions. These were: (1) a tariff war against Serbia when the latter refused to accept an economically dependent position, (2) the outright annexation of Bosnia-Hercegovina, and (3) a projected railroad across the Sandjak of Novipazar, a narrow strip of land separating Serbia and Montenegro. When these actions proved insufficient to weaken Serbia, Vienna sought (in the main successfully) to deny to Serbia and to Montenegro significant fruits of their victories (against Turkey) in the Balkan wars of 1912-1913. Even this was not enough. Consequently, the rulers in Vienna decided on an outright military attack, which came in the summer of 1914.

As noted earlier, the tariff war lasted from 1906 to 1911, and did not have the effect that Vienna desired.[19] The task of finding new outlets for Serbia's trade was not easy for a government operating a relatively new and fragile democratic political system, but in the end victory was achieved. The tariff war tested the resourcefulness of the Serbs, strengthened their self-confidence, and lifted their morale. While plans for promoting Serbia's economic growth had to be curtailed during the tariff war, in the process doors were opened to new foreign capital, which in the end contributed significantly to Serbia's economic development.

In the annexation of Bosnia-Hercegovina, however, Austria-Hungary had her way.[20] She had been given the right to occupy and administer the region by the Congress of Berlin (1878), but not to annex it. By 1908, however, she had gone a long way toward getting German and Russian blessings for the annexation. The announcement of the actual act in October of that year came while the Serbian leaders were preoccupied with the tariff war. For Serbia, the annexation

struck at vital national interests more than the tariff war, and the reaction among the people was in the nature of a suicidal frenzy, demanding war. The leaders in Belgrade knew, however, that little Serbia
could do no more than protest. Serbia's stand was juridically unassail-
able; France, England and Russia agreed, but were unwilling to act.
Russia even exerted pressure on the Serbian government, forcing it
to declare in writing that Serbia's rights were not impaired by the
annexation, and agreeing to cease further protests.

Austria's plan to annex Bosnia-Hercegovina and to build a railway across Novipazar were planned at about the same time, with the
latter due to come first. Austria-Hungary's presence in Novipazar
was based on the Treaty of Berlin, as indicated above, and she was
anxious to gain the right to build the railway before she would tear
up that treaty with the annexation. By controlling a piece of territory
stretching from Bosnia-Hercegovina to Salonika, Austria-Hungary
would have direct access to Bulgaria, and would thus encircle Serbia
and keep her from reaching the Adriatic, Montenegro, or even Greece.
When the railway project was announced in January 1908, there was
a general public outcry in Europe. Serbia's leaders, at that time
engaged in talks with Vienna concerning a new trade agreement, did
not protest publicly. Subsequently, the Young Turk revolution in
Turkey doomed the project, and Vienna was thereby spared considerable embarrassment.

At about the time that the tariff war ended (1911), the Balkan
nations were working on an agreement (actually signed early in 1912),
to liberate their region from Turkish control. The war broke out in
October 1912, and the Turks met a quick defeat. This came as a sur-
prise to most of Europe, and especially to the leaders in Vienna, who
had anticipated that Turkey would administer a defeat to the upstart
Balkan nations. Responding to Turkey's call for intervention by the
Great Powers, Austria-Hungary demanded that Serbian and Monte-
negrin forces be forced to withdraw—they had both driven to the
Adriatic. The Serbian leader, Pašić, was in a difficult spot; the people
and army officers were publicly defiant. But since the Russian foreign
minister, Sazonov, promised to defend Serbia's interests, Pašić placed
the matter in the hands of the Great Powers. Much to the chagrin of
Montenegro's and Serbia's leaders, the Great Powers decided to create
an Albanian state on the Adriatic, denying to the Serbian states their
hard-fought-for victories.

Serbia also had difficulties with Bulgaria as to where their new
boundary should be. In their agreement before entering the war
against Turkey, the two nations had agreed that the Russian Tsar

would arbitrate in case of unresolved conflict. Since Bulgaria seemed in no mood to seek a peaceful solution, concentrating her troops on Serbia's borders, Pašić finally agreed to ask the Tsar to arbitrate, although he was apprehensive because of Russia's pro-Bulgarian policy in the past. With great difficulty, he got the approval of the Skupština in support of his position. While still in the Skupština, however, he received news that the Bulgarian forces had launched an attack against Serbia on all fronts. Fortunately for Serbia, the Bulgarians had not only alienated the Rumanians but had also attacked the Greeks. Within a month the Bulgarians were defeated, and a peace treaty was signed in Bucharest in August 1913.

Serbia's prime minister, Nikola Pašić, was more perceptive than other European rulers in his conviction that the rulers in Vienna were planning additional hostile acts against his country. In the early spring of 1914, he expressed his fears personally to the Russian Tsar in Petrograd, and asked his help in case of an Austro-Hungarian attack. Because the Tsar was incredulous, Pašić reviewed in detail the events of the previous several years, pointing out that the rulers in Vienna no doubt viewed most of these events as defeats for them, and would no doubt engage in other actions, including a military attack. The Tsar listened but was still disbelieving. In the end, however, he promised Russian protection in case of an unprovoked attack. With this assurance, Pašić decided to hold new elections in the summer, particularly since the general elections of 1912 had given his party an exceedingly narrow majority.

Pašić's fears proved justified. The Austro-Hungarian leaders decided that a preventive war against Serbia was an absolute necessity for the salvation of the dual monarchy, and succeeded in convincing their allies in Berlin of this position.[21] This was before the assassination in Sarajevo of the heir to the Austrian throne in June 1914, which the Vienna rulers used as pretext a month later to declare war on Serbia. While the assassination was the work of Austria's Serbian subjects in Bosnia-Hercegovina, there is no proof that the Serbian government even had any knowledge of the assassination plans, let alone having any part in them. Nevertheless, Vienna on July 23 presented the Serbs with an unbelievably humiliating 48-hour ultimatum, drafted in such a way that Serbia could not accept it and still remain an independent state.

Most Serbian politicians, including Pašić, were on the campaign trail when the ultimatum was presented in Belgrade. In no position to go to war with anyone, Serbia's leaders were compelled to accept practically all the demands, and expressed a willingness to refer the other matters to the International Court at the Hague. Indicative of how little Vienna was interested in the Serbian answer is the fact that after a hasty reading of the note that Pašić handed him, the Austro-Hungarian minister declared that diplomatic relations between their two countries were being broken. Moreover, he and his staff, bags already packed, were on the evening train within two hours after Pašić had handed him the Serbian answer.

No one had expected little Serbia to be much of a match for the Austro-Hungarian empire. Yet the latter's armies, after some initial victories, were badly beaten by the Serbs in several important battles. In less than a year all Serbian soil was cleared of the enemy. But in the summer of 1915, a coordinated German-Austrian campaign (subsequently joined by Bulgaria) was launched against the Serbian forces, compelling them to withdraw. Ultimately the remnants of the Serbian armies made their way across the Albanian mountains in the winter of 1915-1916, ending up on the Greek island of Corfu.[22] There were heavy losses in men and materiel, made worse by the terrible epidemic of typhus. By April 1916, however, the Serbs (with Allied help) had re-equipped an army of some 115,000 men, which was sent to the Salonika front. It should also be noted that it was on Corfu that the basic agreements were reached concerning the creation of Yugoslavia, which was consummated on December 1, 1918, and subsequently gained widespread recognition in the Versailles peace settlement.

It is interesting to note that in a brief historical period Serbia made great strides toward consolidating a liberal-democratic political system. In the decade before World War I constitutional liberalism and parliamentary supremacy made greater headway in Serbia than in other European countries, except that certain countries, such as Great Britain, must be excluded from any such comparison. According to one foreign observer, Serbia on the eve of the First World War was "the most democratic country in Europe."[23] And her progress was achieved at a time of difficult domestic and foreign problems. To be sure, cabinets were characterized by an element of instability, with the average life of a cabinet being eight and one-half months, but often a new cabinet was a reshuffle, with the principal personalities continuing for longer periods of time. All things considered, political democracy was in a state of excellent health in pre-World War I Serbia.

X

THE MILITARY AND POLITICAL DEVELOPMENT

In the process of regaining her independence and developing her own political institutions, Serbia experienced a number of crises, domestic and foreign. In the course of these events, the armed forces played an important role, but they never assumed power or established a military dictatorship even for a brief period. The burden of what follows is to describe the role played by the army and to suggest some reasons for the absence of a military take-over in Serbia.

The Army and the Overthrow of the Obrenović Dynasty

Although there was no standing army in Serbia until late in the century, a large part of the peasantry had guns. All armed persons constituted a potential citizen army, usually responding to the commands of local leaders. There were only a few garrisons in being at any one time, the main one being in the city of Kragujevac, which was the capital of Serbia until 1841.

In the wake of the creation in 1838 of the Council, which seemed to threaten the authority of Prince Miloš, army leaders in Kragujevac sent him a letter in which they criticized the Council and offered their assistance. Miloš responded by saying that help was not needed. Nevertheless, certain of these forces began moving toward Belgrade. One of Miloš's strong men, and a member of the Council, Toma Vučić Perišić (usually known simply as Vučić) met these men with armed units. When the would-be rebels against the Council saw what was in store for them, they laid down their arms.[1] Ironically, Vučić had a plan to oust Miloš, and succeeded in turning the army against him, forcing him to abdicate in 1839.[2]

Vučić and other members of the Council, who came to be known collectively as the Defenders of the Constitution (the Turkish *hati-sherif* which had given them considerable power), were determined not to let Miloš's son Mihailo (a minor) and his supporters get the upper hand. Vučić paid special attention to the army. As an effective demagogue, on one of his visits to the barracks, he spoke to the soldiers as follows:

> I am not afraid of anyone: not of the Prince nor of the Council, not of ministers or bishops. And no one should be afraid of any one. We are all equal; Prince and swineherd, swineherd and Councilor, Councilor and merchant, merchant and judge. . . . It should not be that some warm themselves in the sun while the rest of us stay in the shade, and that only one lifts his head high and the

rest of us look down at the ground. All of us should lift our
heads high and be warmed by the sun. I am not afraid of any one,
only of the constitution, and I will say that to Prince Mihailo
just as I said it to his father. . . . If he does not abide by the constitution, I will force him out just as I did his father. . . . Let no
one think that the Prince can do as he wishes in the nation; he
must obey the people and do what the people want.[3]

Nevertheless, Mihailo's supporters succeeded in forcing Vučić
and his followers to leave Serbia for a time, but they were back in
less than two years.[4] As soon as they returned they sought to fan
dissatisfaction among the people.[5]

Vučić, perhaps the first man in Serbian history to drag the army
into political quarrels, planned and organized a revolt against Mihailo.
He executed his plan by bribing the commander of the garrison in
Kragujevac, as well as the man in charge of munitions.[6] In this way
he gained control of the army and the principal munitions stores, including the available cannons. It is agreed that Mihailo had ten times
as many men available as Vučić, but he did not want to shed the
blood of innocent men, and therefore lacked the will to use them.[7]
But it should not be forgotten that Vučić had control of the cannons,
and that the order to some units to resist Vučić had been burned.

Vučić also practiced psychological warfare. He often said that
he was not against the Prince, that he came to free him from his
ministers. Moreover, in the initial firing of the cannons which over-
looked Kragujevac, a number of persons were killed. In the night
Vučić had the heads cut off from the corpses and had these placed
on stakes along the road that his troops would pass. When they passed
along that road the next day, Vučić said to the people and to his troops:
"There brothers, see what that dog [Prince Mihailo] did. . . ."[8]

Before long Mihailo fled the country. In popular parlance,
"Vučić's cannons decided the quarrel between the Prince and the
Defenders of the Constitution."[9] But it was the latter that assumed
power and not the military.

The Army and the Revolution of 1858

After nearly twenty years of oligarchic rule, the Skupština (parliament) overthrew the Prince (Alexander Karadjordjević) and the
Council in 1858 in what was the most peaceful revolution in Serbian
history. The army, however, played a passive role, although the threat
that it might be used continued for two or three days.[10] It sat in the
barracks almost directly across the road from the building in which
the Skupština sessions were being held.

The fact that the army did not get involved can in large measure be credited to the minister of interior, Ilija Garašanin. At that time there was no war ministry; the army was run by the military section of the ministry of interior. By a fortunate move, Garašanin, a shrewd member of the Council, helped the Prince to go to the Turkish fortress for protection, thereby separating the Prince from the army, and thereby making himself the master of the bayonets.[11]

Although the Skupština ousted the Prince and the Council, and invited Miloš Obrenović to return, Garašanin refused to turn over the command of the army and the police except to a provisional government.[12] An agreement was reached and bloodshed was avoided.

There were other considerations that prevented the army from getting involved. At a critical moment a large mass of people had gathered around the Skupština building, and virtually bare-handedly imposed itself between the Skupština and the barracks. The military commanders did not dare to order the army to fire into the crowd without orders from someone above. Moreover, the head of the military section of the ministry of interior, Milivoje Blaznavac (of whom we shall hear later), was in the barracks, and was kept in check by a flow of notes from Garašanin. And, as we have seen, the Prince demonstrated that he would rather flee than order the army to shoot.

The Army and the Choice of Mihailo's Successor

Prince Mihailo was assassinated in 1868, but he had no real heir. A hastily formed regency decided that a Large National Skupština should choose a successor. But Blaznavac, who had become minister of war in 1865, decided the question the next day in favor of a grand-nephew of Mihailo's (Milan Obrenović), then a boy of 14 living in Paris. Blaznavac, viewing himself as the savior of the Obrenović dynasty, proclaimed Milan the new Prince, and got the army to take an oath of loyalty to him. This military coup was subsequently ratified by the Large National Skupština.[13]

A biographical note on Blaznavac is interesting.[14] His political career began when he burned an order to use the army against Vučić's rebels in 1842. For this he got fifty lashes, but after Vučić's victory he was given a job in the ministry of interior, and in 1848 he became an adjutant of Prince Alexander Karadjordjević. He was in France at the time of the coup by Louis Napoleon, and witnessed what a man of daring could do with the help of the army. He came back to Serbia impressed with the power of bayonets.

Blaznavac was in a position to play a significant role in 1858, at which time he held the rank of colonel, the highest rank in the Serbian army. As we have seen above, however, he spent the three days of the revolution in the barracks as an observer of events. He did not dare to move except by order of his minister, Garašanin. When Miloš came back as Prince in January 1859, Blaznavac was sent back to his village.

Although Miloš's son, Mihailo, had said that Blaznavac would never become a minister while he was Prince, Blaznavac became minister of war in 1865. He knew how to manipulate people. He got the support of Anka Konstantinović, and she had influence with Mihailo, who was in love with her daughter Katarina.[15]

In the three-member regency which was created after Mihailo's death, Blaznavac was known as First Regent.[16] Ironically, this was also the beginning of his decline as a political force. He prepared a draft of a law that would have made him supreme commander of the army during the Prince's minority, but the Skupština refused to pass it. Rather, it passed a resolution to the effect that the supreme command would be in the hands of all three regents.[17]

When Prince Milan became of age, Blaznavac's position improved for a time. He became president of the council of ministers and minister of war. Also, he was made a general, a rank which no one had held until that time. Just when he seemed to be gaining in influence again, he died unexpectedly in 1873.

The Army Under Milan

Prince Milan, although only 19, took advantage of the death of Blaznavac to place control of the army in his own hands. He indicated that he would always demand that the minister of war be more dependent upon him than upon the cabinet.[18] This rule was in force during the regimes of Milan and his son Alexander, a reign that was ended in 1903, as we have seen, by the military.

Milan wanted the whole officer corps to be made up of his personal friends and supporters. He abolished the citizen army in 1883, and sought to make the standing army the principal pillar of the dynasty.[19] The atttempt to take arms away from the people led to the Timok Rebellion, which was brutally put down. Since the largest political party in the nation, the Radical party, was blamed for the rebellion, many of its leaders were executed and the party's activities were severly limited for several years.

Even so, Milan could not govern without the Radicals, although he made sure that persons loyal to him held the key positions. In one ministry of seven persons, three were active army officers and two were reservists.[20] Before he abdicated in 1889, Milan had arranged to appoint the three regents, two of whom were generals through whom he could continue to play a role in Serbian politics.[21] During the latter years of his son's reign, Milan was back in Serbia as commandant of the army.[22]

In the words of Slobodan Jovanović:

> Blaznavac was the first to successfully utilize the army for the solution of domestic political questions, and his example was contagious. . . . The history of Milan's son Alexander has beginning and closing chapters in an officers' conspiracy. . . . The Topčider catastrophe [Mihailo's assassination] . . . proclaimed the entry of the army into our internal politics.[23]

Civil-Military Relations After 1903

The Obrenović dynasty, which became exceedingly unpopular at home, had also regaled Europe with the scandalous behavior of its most important members. In 1903, a conspiracy in the army served to end the dynasty in cold blood. The conspirators immediately turned power over to the parliament, which invited Peter Karadjordjević to come to the throne. The democratic constitution of 1888 was brought back and Serbia again became a parliamentary and constitutional monarchy. But the predominance of the civil authority was not accepted without question.

Several questions seemed to aggravate civil-military relations in the period 1903-1918, and they cannot be discussed adequately here. One was the question of the conspirators, some of whom had to be retired as a price of international recognition, a solution insisted upon mainly by England. Although an acceptable solution was found, dissatisfaction in the army was to simmer, especially among the nationalistically inclined officers who in 1911 founded the Union or Death organization. Generally known as the "Black Hand," this organization was dedicated to work for the union with Serbia of lands populated mainly by Serbs but then under foreign rule, mainly under Turkey and Austro-Hungary. This organization was convinced that Serbian politicians were not working actively enough in the pursuit of this goal. In subsequent years, the ostensible influence of this group of army officers served to produce a counter-group of military men, the so-called "White Hand."

A second question that aggravated civil-military relations concerned the administration of the newly acquired areas following the Balkan Wars of 1912-1913. This question was to have been a major issue in the electoral campaign of 1914, which had been launched shortly before the Austro-Hungarian declaration of war against Serbia, but the war caused the election to be postponed. Serbia's military successes in the first year of the war served to blunt the issue, but the tragedy of the retreat of the remnants of the Serbian army across Albania in the winter of 1915-1916 was a source of bitter recrimination. Some Serbian military commanders believed that the army could have been spared the severe losses if the political leaders had early enough permitted them to attack the Bulgarian forces in the direction of Salonika.

The culmination of the civil-military conflict occurred in Salonika in 1917, at a time when the Serbian army, along with Allied troops, was fighting its way back into the homeland. A number of officers were brought to trial in Salonika before a military court on charges of attempting to overthrow Prince Regent Alexander and the duly constituted Government. As reported in the previous chapter, eleven were found guilty, with some receiving death sentences and others prison terms. Moreover, in the wake of the trial a large number of officers were retired or demoted.

The Salonika Trial and its consequences have been the subject of many books and countless articles.[24] There are still many unresolved questions as to the guilt or innocence of those tried, the appropriateness of the penalties, and the motives of the principals on both sides. It would seem clear, however, that the monarch and his ministers were convinced that a settling of accounts between the civil and military authorities could not be avoided or delayed. Whether they were right in their judgment is another matter.

Some Concluding Remarks

In seeking an explanation for the absence of a military takeover in Serbia, several factors deserve consideration, and not necessarily in the order of their importance. First of all, Serbia was a land of homogeneous people, with no sharp national or religious differences. The people were ethnically and culturally united.[25] Nation-building, or rebuilding, after more than 400 years of Turkish rule, was made less difficult by virtue of the fact that a sense of national identity had been maintained. When the Serbs began their struggle for independence in the first part of the 19th century, the people were motivated by the struggle for independence and by a continuing desire to liberate their brother Serbs in adjoining lands. In short, there were no national or tribal groups in Serbia that sought separation, no elements who might see in the military a needed protector.

Secondly, and closely related, there were no sharp class differences in Serbia. In the Serbia of the middle ages, there was a nobility, but, as noted earlier, it was liquidated by the Turks. During the critical years (1815-1838) of his rule, Prince Miloš did not permit the establishment of feudal landholdings, and thereby enabled Serbia to become a nation of small landholders. No new nobility could arise, with the result that a sense of equality was pervasive. Even the more well-to-do peasants still thought of themselves as peasants and not as gentlemen. When certain class differences did become evident around the turn of the century, they were not of such nature that military support would flow to one or the other side.

Thirdly, Serbia as a peasant society, was inhospitable to the army's becoming a military class. In the course of establishing independence for Serbia in the 1820s and 1830s, Prince Miloš, out of fear of the Turks, did not take arms away from the peasants. Free of a landowning nobility, and armed, the peasant could hardly escape being the main political force in an agrarian land such as Serbia. All regimes had to take this into account. After the formation of political parties, and especially after the Radical party had become the party of the peasants, King Milan in 1883 sought to take arms away from the peasants, and to replace the citizens' army with a standing army. This provoked a bloody rebellion, which was brutally put down, but the peasant masses were not to be denied. Whenever the elections were free, prior to the final establishment of a constitutional parliamentary democracy in 1903, the Radical party always won an overwhelming majority.

Fourthly, a basic democratic spirit among the Serbs was inhospitable to a military dictatorship. There was a visible demonstration of this spirit even before Serbia was fully independent of the Turks. Under Karadjordje and under Miloš, a Council was established to limit the powers of the ruler. As the 19th century moved on, there was a determined struggle to establish democratic political institutions. Within less than six years of Milan's suppression of the peasant rebellion in 1883, he found it necessary (or prudent) to acquiesce in the inauguration of a democratic parliamentary regime, and to abdicate as king. Although Milan had sought to build up a military caste, and with some success, the loyalty was a personal one. His bitter disagreements with his son Alexander, his death in 1901, and the failure of Alexander and his cabinets to gain the respect of the people (including the army), led to an army officers' conspiracy that wiped out the Obrenović dynasty in 1903, and paved the way for the Radical party to come to power and to establish a constitutional monarchy under Peter Karadjordjević I.

Finally, the principle that a military man should be politically neutral seems to have taken root early in Serbia. The ministry of war was invariably headed by an army officer, precisely because of the belief that a political leader in that post might be tempted to use the army for partisan political purposes. In 1892, for example, the cabinet's program was signed by all ministers except the minister of war. Moreover, Serbian laws forbade political activity by military men, who did not even have the right to vote. When in this century the military began to get involved in politics, encouraged in part by the political opponents of the Radical party, the result was that politics came into the army, dividing many of the officers into two hostile groups. In the end, the civil-military conflict that ensued led to a settling of accounts at the Salonika trial in 1917.[26]

XI
CONCLUSION

The Serbs, as the previous chapters have demonstrated, achieved a stable democratic political system in the course of the nineteenth century. Considering that a substantial part of those one hundred years was required to gain, first autonomy and then independence, and having in view that the Serbs were emerging from nearly five hundred years of Turkish colonial rule, considering further the general backwardness of the area and the less than rapid tempo of the nineteenth century as compared to the twentieth, it can be said that the political development of nineteenth century Serbia was rather intensive. This achievement was all the more outstanding in view of domestic and foreign obstacles, and in view of the fact that political development in certain western European countries (e.g., Germany) proceeded more slowly than in Serbia. What factors or considerations can help us to explain Serbia's impressive political development? There would appear to be several.

One was the political culture of Serbia. As the Serbs began the process of winning independence there was no appreciable problem in nation-building or of national identity. Even under long years of Turkish rule, significant portions of each generation were socialized in terms of their nation's past glory and in the notion that Serbia would again be an independent state. This socialization, as indicated elsewhere, was performed in the main by bards and religious leaders, who were important communicators of social and other values. The result was that there was a widespread sense of popular identification with the history, territory, and national identity of Serbia. This deeply-rooted and stable psychological orientation of the people was quite unlike the situation that exists in fragmented political cultures. Not only did the Serbs have no difficulty in making the state and nation coincide (unlike the Germans or Italians), they in fact succeeded in having their nationalism transformed to a type of ideology.

Another favorable aspect of Serbia's political culture was the absence of sharp class or social differences. By contrast with many western European nations, Serbia was not stuck with old feudal social structures that had to be destroyed. The Turks had done away with the Serbian nobility and aristocracy, and had therefore eliminated virtually all class differences among the Serbs. There were well-to-do peasants, to be sure, but the social gap between the rulers and the ruled was minimal. The relative equality may have been more psychological than real, but it was important in the acceptance of legitimacy of the evolving Serbian leadership. The new ruling elite had close ties with the peasantry, even though in time dissatisfaction did grow.

Moreover, Serbia's political culture was free of regional or ethnic differences. The population was ethnically and religiously compact; the few non-Serbs were easily assimilated. There were no secessionist movements or vassal armies to contend with. There were local and regional loyalties, but it was not too difficult to transfer these to national loyalties, in large part because the dream of national resurrection during Turkish rule had not faded. All in all, Serbia's historical heritage made it possible for nation-building to come before industrialization or even before the advent of anything approaching sophisticated methods of political communication. Contrary to the Deutsch thesis, urbanism and nationalism are not closely related in the Serbian experience.

A second factor that helps to explain Serbia's political development is that the Serbs had some sense or feel for democracy. This can be seen in some respects in the clan organization out of which grew peasant assemblies even in Turkish times. Abstract discussion of alternative courses of action, values, etc., would have been difficult, if not impossible, early in the nineteenth century. Yet during the uprising under Karadjordje several assemblies were convened, giving those who participated some opportunity to state their views. There was a type of patriarchal authoritative decision-making, combined with imperfect yet meaningful consultation. Only late in the century was it possible to have reasonably rational discussion of alternative programs, particularly in relation to the experiences of other European states. But the people's deep awareness of political problems, and their expectation that some form of consultation would occur, made the establishment of democratic political institutions virtually inevitable.

The people's attitude was manifest in their great interest in politics, and in their efforts to be informed. Much of their information came in oral discussion and conversation, out of which there seems to have grown a respect for learning and intellectuals. At times the people were misinformed, but the important thing to note is their desire to be informed. This suggests that in a small state where political problems are not overly complex the need of formal education, even literacy, is not so important as sometimes assumed. In the latter half of the nineteenth century the Serbs had a widespread interest and involvement in the political system, though not necessarily always in the decision-making aspects thereof. This became increasingly important as Serbia became a truly functioning democracy after 1903.

A third factor that helps us to understand Serbia's political development was the surfacing of determined, and in large part respected, political leaders.[1] In the first decades of the nineteenth century there were Karadjordje and Miloš, who were the unquestioned leaders of the two uprisings, in both a military and political sense. Although admittedly authoritarian, they were faced with demands for some participation in policy making. Because of his failure to heed these demands, Miloš was driven from his position as hereditary prince. He was replaced by a group of his opponents who inaugurated a period of oligarchic rule. Nevertheless they provided decisive leadership toward a rudimentary modernization of Serbia's legal, administrative and educational system. Following their overthrow, the decisive leadership came from Prince Mihailo, who further modernized the Serbian state, although it was done through an enlightened despotism.

In a way the rule of Mihailo represented a transition period, because after him no political leadership in Serbia was accepted as legitimate without serious challenge unless it had a popular base. It was following Mihailo's reign that political parties evolved, giving to the populace an opportunity to aggregate around leaders of the party that was perceived as most closely representing their respective interests. In the last two decades of the century, it was the Radical party and its leader, Nikola Pašić, who captured the support of Serbia's peasant masses. In a word, decisive leadership was transferred from the monarch to the leaders of political parties, notably the Radical party, even though kings Milan and Alexander were able to delay it for a time. In large part because of their failure to recognize political realities, their dynasty came to an end in 1903. After that there was never any serious questioning of the principle that political leadership was to be in the hands of the leaders who could command a majority in parliament.

In the post-1903 period there are countless examples of a dedication to and respect for constitutionalism and high principles in political behavior. Two examples may be cited as illustrative. At the time of the Serbian cabinet's decision in 1915 to go into exile with the Serbian military forces, the aged King Peter I told his ministers that he would stay behind with his people. When informed that where he was there also was the government and the nation, he asked if this was according to the constitution. Informed in the affirmative, he asked to see the document, but was told that whereas the constitution did not say so explicitly, it clearly implied it. His response: if going into exile with his cabinet was the constitutional thing to do, he would go.

The other example is one of adherence to a code of high personal principles in politics. In 1912 the leader of the Independent Radical party, Ljubomir Stojanović, was asked by the King to form a cabinet. He agreed in principle but he told the King that he must first consult with the caucus of his party's parliamentary deputies. Following Stojanović's report to the caucus there was some discussion. One deputy, with good intentions but a little heatedly, spoke some critical words: "It is easy for you Belgraders, the policeman salutes you but down below he beats us. . . . It is easy for you Ljubo, with a large pension and down here there is starvation. . . . The party has given you . . . ."[2] In the noisy surroundings some heard these words and some did not. Stojanović, it seems, heard them. He got up and left, never to return, despite the pleas of some of his high party colleagues. He resigned as party leader, and gave up all of his other positions, including the pension he had had as a university professor. He was left without any regular income, and for the remainder of his life he existed on exceedingly meager means. The example of Stojanović may be the most dramatic, but that it occurred at all is at least indicative of the high level that Serbian politics had reached on the eve of World War I.

When a few years ago F. M. Barnard concluded that "political development, in the last analysis, is an act of will," he could have had Serbian leaders in mind, although I am sure he knew nothing of them.[3] Serbian leaders, both the authoritarian and the democratic ones, seemed to have confidence in the rightness of what they were doing. They were advocate-leaders, who set major goals for their people, and who were not afraid to harness resources in the pursuit of those goals. And the people, although they recognized the need for leadership, did not abdicate their rights to discuss and to pass judgment.

A fourth factor that sheds light on Serbia's political development is the more or less successful struggle to institutionalize political processes and practices, so that political decisions would be made through rational and secular procedures. One phase of this struggle was the concept that the highest law-giver should be the Skupština, an assembly to be freely elected by the people. A second phase of this struggle rested on the assumption that political parties are the appropriate institutions to provide the electorate with alternate sets of political leaders and competing political programs.

The concept of a popular assembly (skupština) can be traced back to the clan organization of the Serbian empire of the Middle Ages, although there is no evidence that such assemblies were looked upon as legislative bodies. The basic notion was that there should be consultation, and for a long time Serbian assemblies were consultative bodies only. Before the end of Miloš's reign in the 1830s, however, there were demands for an assembly (Skupština) that would have legislative powers. As the preceding chapters indicate, this demand was not rapidly satisfied, and indeed was not fully realized until late in the 19th century. It should also be noted that as more and more importance was accorded the Skupština by the forces of democracy, the principle of ministerial responsibility was insisted upon, so that ministers could stay in office only so long as they had the confidence of the Skupština. Correspondingly, the monarch was denied real political power, which was transferred to the popularly elected assembly.

The development of political parties in Serbia served to institutionalize political struggles and to channel political differences so as not to tear the society apart. Fortuitously perhaps, Serbian parties evolved during the critical decades of the last century in such a way as to be conducive to democratic development, i.e., few parties.[4] Moreover, there was one strong party which was capable of defining and realizing public interests, thus becoming a key agent of legitimacy and stability.[5]

Even before the development of political parties there were two rough coalitions around which opposing elements could coalesce, indeed a type of primitive two-party system. These were the supporters of the Obrenović and Karadjordjević dynasties, who after the restoration of the Obrenovićes in 1858 were two distinct political camps. This arrangement tended to channel opposition even though it did not domesticate it. The formation and establishment of political parties, which was nearly always identifiable with one or the other dynasty, served to domesticate opposition in that elections provided a peaceful mode of expressing the people's feelings. It is true that at times when official actions made the elections something less than free or fair, there was the danger that a more virulent conflict might erupt, as indeed one did. Nevertheless the danger of violent conflict was seemingly minimized by the expectation that the next elections would be different, and increasingly they were. After 1903, however, no one seriously questioned the fairness or freedom of Serbian elections.

In the growth and institutionalization of political parties, Serbia achieved a rational type of legitimacy. This was especially true as the Radical party became the overwhelming favorite of the electorate. Moreover, Serbian politics generally assumed an increasingly rational tone. While the Serbian Orthodox Church was the state church, this fact did not prevent members of other faiths from holding high political office. For example, around the turn of the century Jovan Djaja, a Roman Catholic, was minister of education, as was Ljubomir Klerić, a protestant, who was also minister of the economy. In essence, the people elected representatives to the Skupština, and the leaders of the majority party determined the nation's political course and managed the administration of public affairs.

The foregoing factors would seem to this writer to go a long way in explaining why the Serbian political system had achieved, in the decade prior to World War I, a capacity to deal in a democratic way with the domestic and international environment. It had, in the words of Samuel P. Huntington, managed to establish a critical relationship between political participation and political institutionalization without worrying about the issues of which should be labelled "political development."[6] In short, the system possessed the appropriate mix of the ingredients that we usually associate with a relatively stable democratic political order, and it is hoped that the above discussion will have shed some light on the elements that shaped the Serbian political system.

FOOTNOTES

Introduction

1. Nikola Radojčić, *Srpski državni sabori u srednjem veku* [Serbian State Assemblies in the Middle Ages] (Belgrade, 1940), 3-4. Much of this information is fragmentary and much was read into it by European historians.

2. Sometimes it was king, prince, or despot. See Georgije Ostrogorski, *Istorija Vizantije* (Belgrade, 1959), 538-39.

3. For a critical discussion, see Radojčić, *ibid.*, 7-33. He insists that a number of noted historians, including Jireček, Taranovski, *et al.*, made serious errors in their discussion of medieval Serbia.

4. Radojčić, *ibid.*, 104ff, 193ff. There is some evidence that men under arms participated.

5. *Ibid.*, 211ff, 259ff.

6. *Ibid.*, 304.

7. *Ibid.*, 306.

8. *Ibid.*, 158-83. Apparently there was considerable disunity at this time in the church and among the nobility.

9. *Ibid.*, 301-02.

10. For an interesting article, see Aleksandar Solovjev, "Pojam države u srednjevekovnoj Srbiji" [The idea of the state in medieval Serbia], *Godišnica Nikole Čupića*, VLII (1933), 64-92.

11. Probably the best work on the subject is Stojan Novaković, *Zakonik Stefan Dušana cara srpskog 1349 i 1354* [Law Code of Serbian Tsar Stefan Dušan 1349 and 1354] (Belgrade, 1898). Part one was issued in 1349 and part two in 1354. Also see Jevrem Gerasimović, *Staro Srpsko pravo* [Ancient Serbian law] (Belgrade, 1925).

12. Gerasimović, *ibid.*, 161.

13. See Stanoje Stanojević, *Iz naše prošlosti* [From Our Past] (Belgrade, 1934), especially 5ff and 61ff. Also see Svetolik M. Grebenac, *Kroz istoriju Srba* [Through the History of the Serbs] (Belgrade, 1938), 3-26.

14. Radojčić, *ibid.*, 31-33.

15. Much of what follows is based on an exceedingly interesting pamphlet by Dragoljub Jovanović, *Socialna struktura Srbije* (Belgrade, 1932). This pamphlet was reprinted from *Srpski književni glasnik* (March 1 and 16, 1932).

16. The best work on general conditions of Serbian life in the early part of the 19th century is Tihomir R. Djordjević, *Iz Sribje Kneza Miloša* [From the Serbia of Prince Miloš] (2 vols., Belgrade, 1922, 1924). The first volume deals with cultural situations and the second with demography.

17. *Statistički godišnjak kr. Srbije, 1898-1899* [Statistical Year-book] (Belgrade, 1900), VI, 202-04.

18. For an interesting discussion of Serbia's politico-economic problems, see the speeches and treatises of the one-time Radical party minister of the national economy, Kosta Stojanović, *Govori i rasprave: političko-ekonomske* [Speeches and treatises] (Belgrade, 1910, 1911), 2 vols. For a Yugoslav Marxist view, see Dragoslav Janković, *O političkim strankama u Srbji XIX veka* [Concerning Political Parties in 19th Century Serbia] (Belgrade, 1951), 129-79.

19. Two works by Serbian writers are especially pertinent. They are: Grgur Jakšić, *Evropa i vaskrs Srbije (1804-1834)* [Europe and the resurrection of Serbia] (Belgrade, 1933), and Vasilj Popović, *Evropa i srpsko pitanje u periodu oslobodjenja, 1804-1918* [Europe and the Serbian question in the period of liberation] (Belgrade, 1938).

Chapter II

1. *The Memoirs of Prota Matija Nenadović*, edited and translated by Lovett F. Edwards (Oxford, 1969), 167.

2. The fact that Rodofinikin was Greek made him all the more suspicious in Karadjordje's eyes.

3. The definitive work on the period is Mihailo Gavrilović, *Miloš Obrenović* (3 vols., Belgrade, 1908, 1909, 1912). The third volume ends with coverage of events through 1835. The manuscript of the fourth and final volume was lost during the retreat of the Serbian armies across Albania in the First World War. Another indispensable work is Mita Petrović, *Financije i ustanove obnovljene Srbije do 1842* [Finance and institutions of restored Serbia to 1842] (3 vols., Belgrade, 1897, 1898, 1899). For an account of the conditions in 1815 and a depiction of the revolt, see Gavrilović, I, 132-238.

4. For an excellent commentary, see Slobodan Jovanović, *Iz naše istorije i književnosti* [From our history and literature] (Belgrade, 1931), 3-34. This was originally published in *Srpski književni glasnik* in 1909 and 1913 in connection with the publication of the second and third volumes of Gavrilović's work cited above.

5. As indicated earlier, this story is told in great detail by Gavrilovic.

6. Slobodan Jovanović, *ibid.*, 4-5.

7. Gavrilović, II, 268-86. Also see Jovanović, *ibid.*, 6-9.

8. Gavrilović, II, 295-307.

9. *Ibid.*, 311.

10. *Ibid.*, 314. Miloš insisted on being the judge in certain cases, not all of them important, and Miloš was not always consistent in his verdicts. On one occasion he forced a priest to eat the divorce decree which he had granted without Miloš's approval.

11. *Ibid.*, 328.

12. *Ibid.*, 329.

13. *Ibid.*, 333. Miloš was illiterate, but at one point Vuk Karadžić induced him to learn to read and write, but Vuk's enemies turned him away before he had progressed too far.

14. *Ibid.*, 442.

15. *Ibid.*, 287ff.

16. *Ibid.*, 311.

17. *Ibid.*, I, 295ff. Also see II, 501-637, which deal with rebellions and executions.

18. *Ibid.*, I, 321.

19. *Ibid.*, 346ff.

20. For a discussion of the background of some of them, see *ibid.*, II, 443-46.

21. *Ibid.*, 457-61.

22. Slobodan Jovanović, *Političke i pravne rasprave* [Political and legal treatises] (Belgrade, 1932), I, 4.

23. For an excellent brief review of this achievement, see Slobodan Jovanović, *Iz naše istorije*, 26-34.

24. Gavrilović, I, 450. Russia believed that Miloš was in fact limited by the national elders, and thought that the relationship should be legalized and strengthened in the Turkish Hatisherif. Large parts of Gavrilović's three volume work are concerned with Great Power policies with respect to Serbia (see his table of contents).

25. Miloš became wealthy in livestock trading and many other ventures. He received *solicited* gifts and much free labor, and he sold trade and commercial licenses.

26. Grgur Jakšić i Dragoslav Stranjaković, *Srbija od 1813 do 1858 godine* (Belgrade, 1937), 54.

27. See Dragoslav Stranjaković, *Vučićeva buna* [Vučić's rebellion] (Belgrade, 1936), 14-15.

28. See Gavrilović, II, 501-637.

29. *Ibid.*, 331-38. For a discussion of the Djakovo rebellion, see 568ff.

30. Jovanović, *Političke i pravne rasprave*, I, 6.

31. *Ibid.*, 9.

32. Jaša M. Prodanović, *Ustavni razvitak i ustavne borbe u Srbiji* [Constitutional development and constitutional struggles in Serbia] (Belgrade, 1936), 44. For a text of the constitution, see 44-60.

33. Jovanović, *Političke i pravne rasprave*, II, 11.

34. Prodanović, *op. cit.*, 65-67.

35. The full name for the Serbian parliament is *Narodna Skupština* (national assembly), while the name of the constituent assembly is *Velika Narodna Skupština* (literally large national assembly). For a description of the early Serbian assemblies in the nineteenth century see Čedomil Mitrinović and Miloš Brašić, *Jugoslovenske Narodne Skupštine i Sabori* (Belgrade, 1937), 4-14.

36. Prodanović, *op. cit.*, 99.

37. See Dragoslav Stranjaković, *Vučićeva buna*, 6-7.

38. *Ibid.*, 7-9.

39. *Ibid.*, 10-12.

40. The Council called a Skupština in September 1842 to ratify the selection of Karadjordjević as prince. The Porte immediately approved, but Russian objections led to an annulment of the selection. A second Skupština in June 1843 again chose Alexander, and he remained prince of Serbia until he was overthrown by a new Skupština in 1858.

Chapter III

1. For a detailed description of the consolidation of power by the Council, also referred to as the oligarchy and the Defenders of the Constitution, see Dragoslav Stranjaković, *Vučićeva buna* [Vučić's rebellion] (Belgrade, 1936). Perhaps the best single work on the Constitutional Defenders is Slobodan Jovanović, *Ustavobranitelji i njihova vlada, 1838-1858* [The Defenders of the Constitution and their rule] (Belgrade, 1912). Also important is Dragoslav Stranjaković, *Vlada Ustavobranitelja, 1842-1853: unutrašnja i spoljašnja politiki* [Government of the Defenders of the Constitution, 1842-1853: Domestic and foreign policy] (Belgrade, 1932). The latter work is more oriented toward foreign policy than that of Jovanović.

2. Stranjaković, *Vučićeva buna*, 35ff.

3. Jovanović, *op. cit.*, p. 1. For a commentary on some of the members of the Council, see Stranjaković, *Vučićeva buna*, 22-26; 98-132. See also his *Vlada Ustavobranitelja*, 83-88. It is also profitable to consult the index entries in the memoirs of Dimitrije Marinković, *Uspomene i doživljaji Dimitrija Marinkovića, 1846-1869* [The memoirs of . . .] (Belgrade, 1939), edited by Stranjaković.

4. Stranjaković, *Vučićeva buna*, 25.

5. *Ibid.*, 23.

6. *Ibid.*, 54-55. Among the issues raised were: increase in taxes, drop in the value of money, increased pay to the clergy, Serbs from Austria in the civil service.

7. Jovanović, *op. cit.*, 1-5.

8. Some Yugoslav Communist scholars have viewed this as an instrument of the bourgeois class, although admitting that the Civil Code in a way preceded bourgeois development. See, for example, Ružica Guzina, "Istoriski osvrt na karakter i značaj Srpskog gradjanskog zakonika od 1844 godine," [A historical look at the character and meaning of the Serbian Civil Code of 1844] *Istoriski glasnik* (Belgrade, 1949), No. 2, 22-37.

9. Jovanović, *Ustavobranitelji*, 14.

10. *Ibid.*, 15.

11. *Ibid.*, 15-16.

12. *Ibid.*, 26.

13. *Ibid.*, 28-29.

14. Stranjaković, *Vlada*, 40-45.

15. Jovanović, *Ustavobranitelji*, 50.

16. *Ibid.*, 49-50.

17. *Ibid.*, 61-68. See also Jovan Skerlić, *Omladina i njena knji-ževnost* [Youth and its literature] (Belgrade, 1906), 17.

18. *Ibid.*, 69.

19. What follows is based mainly on Jovanović, *op. cit.*, 99-114.

20. Based in the main on Jovanović, *op. cit.*, 117-22. But see also Stranjaković, *Vlada*, 88-104.

21. Presumably they could be removed with the approval of the Porte, but there was some disagreement as to how this provision of the Constitution should be interpreted.

22. Stranjaković, *Vlada*, 88-89.

23. Jovanović, *Ustavobranitelji*, 137-42.

24. *Ibid.*, 139, 146, 153.

25. Stranjaković, *Vlada*, pp. 101-04.

26. For a detailed discussion, see Jovanović, *op. cit.*, 161-91.

27. Jovanović propounds the theory that this is the way oligarchies operate. "Aristocratic collegia do not stir up a rebellion against the tyrant, but kill him in the dark." *Ibid.*, 168.

28. *Ibid.*, 204-06.

29. *Ibid.*, 198-204. Also see Stranjaković, *Vlada*, 175ff.

30. *Ibid.*, 18-81. Vučić had resigned his post earlier but no one had dared to accept his resignation.

31. *Ibid.*, 188-89. For a discussion of the Russian pressure, see 189-204.

32. Jovanović, *Ustavobranitelji*, 198-204.

33. The best and most concise account on the subject is Jovanović, *ibid.*, 213-78. See also comments and documents in Andrija Radenić, *Svetoandrejska Skupština* (Belgrade, 1964).

34. See Jovanović, *op. cit.*, 228ff.

35. *Ibid.*, 238-40. Jovanović does not believe that Garašanin wanted to be prince.

36. *Ibid.*, 242.

37. An extremely valuable source for the study of Serbian politics is Grujić's three volumes of memoirs, *Zapisi Jevrema Grujića* (Belgrade, 1922-1923).

38. *Ibid.*, 251.

39. What follows is largedly based on Jovanović, *op. cit.*, 253-78.

40. The central core or fortresses of cities were still under Turkish control.

Chapter IV

1. There are several good works dealing with this period. The best analytical work is Slobodan Jovanović, *Druga vlada Miloša i Mihaila, 1858-1868* [The second reign of Miloš and Mihailo] (Belgrade, 1923). Much valuable material is to be found in Živan Živanović, *Politička istorija Srbije u drugoj polovini devetnaestog veka* [The political history of Serbia in the second half of the 19th century] (4 vols., Belgrade, 1923-1925), and in Jaša M. Prodanović, *Ustavni razvitak i ustavne borbe u Srbiji* [Constitutional development and constitutional struggles in Serbia] (Belgrade, 1936). Also, see Svetozar Marković, *Srbija na Istoku* [Serbia in the East] (Belgrade, 1892, first published in 1872), and Vasa Čubrilović, *Srbija od 1858 do 1878 godine* (Belgrade, 1938).

2. Jovanović, *Druga vlada*, 46-51.

3. For a discussion of Miloš's actions in the dismissal of civil servants, see *ibid.*, 17-27.

4. *Ibid.*, 34-35.

5. *Ibid.*, 27.

6. *Ibid.*, 56-59. His bitter enemy, Vučić, was imprisoned and died while under detention.

7. *Ibid.*, 73-74.

8. *Ibid.*, 34-40; 79-86.

9. For some examples, see *ibid.*, 83-85.

10. *Ibid.*, 89-92.

11. *Ibid.*, 90.

12. As quoted in Živanović, *Politička istorija*, I, 65.

13. As quoted in Čedomil Mitrinović and Miloš N. Brašić, *Jugoslovenske narodne skupštine i sabori* [Yugoslav national assemblies and diets] (Belgrade, 1937), 67.

14. *Ibid.*

15. Fedor Nikić, *Lokalna uprava Srbije u XIX i XX veku* [Local administration in Serbia in the 19th and 20th centuries] (Belgrade, 1927), 85.

16. Jovanović, *Druga vlada,* 105-06.

17. *Ibid.*, 109-17.

18. *Ibid,* 122-23.

19. For a text of the law, see Mitrinović and Brašić, *op. cit.*, 70-71. Also see discussions in Jovanovic, *op. cit.*, 124-32, and Živanović, I, 76-80.

20. Jovanović, *op. cit.*, 127-28. Also see Živanović, *op. cit.*, 138-56.

21. For a discussion of his efforts to unite various parties or factions, see Jovanović, *op. cit.*, 93-100. Also, see Živanović, *op. cit.*, 60-68.

22. *Ibid.*, 99.

23. *Ibid.*, 190-202. See also the anonymous and strongly critical study, *Pravi pretres propasti velikog suda u Srbiji 1864* [Legal discourse on wrecking the Supreme Court in Serbia 1864] (Novi Sad, 1867).

24. Five of the fifteen judges of the Supreme Court had heard the case and made the ruling.

25. Jovanović, *Druga vlada*, 236-42.

26. *Ibid.*, 186-89.

27. For a discussion of Mihailo's difficulties, see *ibid.*, 243-59.

28. See Živanović, *Politička istorija*, 199-205; Jovanović, *op. cit.*, 260-77. Also interesting is the book by a one-time member of the Council of State, Il. N. Djukanović, *Ubistvo Kneza Mihaila i dogodjaji o kojima se nije smelo govoriti* [The killing of Prince Mihailo and the events about which one could not talk] (Belgrade, 1935).

29. The main conspirators were caught in a day or two, and eventually fourteen were shot.

30. Jovanović, *Druga vlada*, 262-63.

31. *Ibid.*, 277. Also, see his *Vlada Milana Obrenovića* [The reign of Milan Obrenović] (Belgrade, 1934), I, 1-51. Also, see Chapter X, below.

32. *Druga vlada*, 151-52.

Chapter V

1. For text of the constitution, see Jaša M. Prodanović, *Ustavni razvitak i ustaven borbe u Srbiji* [Constitutional development and constitutional struggles in Serbia] (Belgrade, 1936), 185-202. For an excellent discussion, see Slobodan Jovanović, *Vlada Milana Obrenovića* [The reign of Milan Obrenović] (3 vols., Belgrade, 1934), I, 84-134. For a critical view, see Stojan M. Protić, *Odlomci iz ustavne i narodne borbe u Srbiji* [Fragments from constitutional and national struggles in Serbia] (Belgrade, 1912), II, 230-31, 265-67.

2. Jovanović, *op. cit.*, 128.

3. Prodanović, *op. cit.*, 203.

4. Jovanović, *op. cit.*, 286-87.

5. *Ibid.*, 316-35.

6. *Protkoli vanredne Narodne Skupštine, od 2-27 Januara 1874* [Protocols of special session of the National Skupština, January 2-27, 1874], 8-13.

7. *Stenografske beleške Narodne Skupštine za 1874-1875* [Stenographic notes . . .], 183-84.

8. Živan Živanović, *Politička istorija Srbije u drugoj polovini devetnaestog veka* [Political history of Serbia in second half of 19th century] (4 vols., Belgrade, 1923-1925), I, 299ff.

9. As quoted in Živanović, *op. cit.*, II, 50-51.

10. *Ibid.*, 70-71.

11. Jovanović, *Vlada Milana*, I, 438-39.

12. *Ibid.*, 458-67.

13. *Ibid.*, II, 28.

14. *Ibid.*, 199-200.

15. *Ibid.*, 300.

16. For an assessment of Ristić, see Jovanović, *op. cit.*, II, 300-05, and Živanović, *op. cit.*, IV, 140-84.

Chapter VI

1. There are several useful works on Serbian political parties. Among these are: Jaša M. Prodanović, *Istorija Političkih stranaka i struja u Srbiji* [History of political parties and movements in Serbia] (Belgrade, 1947); Živan Mitrović, *Srpske političke stranke* (Belgrade, 1939), Dragoslav Janković, *O političkim strankama u Srbiji XIX veka* [Concerning political parties in Serbia in the 19th century] (Belgrade, 1951). The works of Slobodan Jovanović and Živan Živanović, cited in earlier chapters, contain enormous amounts of information about Serbian political parties.

2. For a first hand account of the activities of the liberals, see the published notes of one of their leaders (Jevrem Grujić), *Zapisi Jevrema Grujića* (Belgrade, 1922-1923), especially book II.

3. For a discussion of their legislative enactments, see Slobodan Jovanović, *Vlada Milana*, III, 163-83.

4. For an excellent study, see Woodward D. McClellan, *Svetozar Marković and the Origins of Balkan Socialism* (Princeton, 1964). Some Yugoslav marxists argue that the Radicals cannot be looked upon as the political heirs of Marković, e.g., Dragoslav Janković, *O političkim strankama*, 227, 246ff. But even Janković (267-69) admits that the Radicals were reasonably consistent in their upholding of constitutionalism, basic political freedoms, etc.).

5. See my *Serbia, Nikola Pašić, and Yugoslavia* (New Brunswick, N.J., 1974).

6. Raša Milošević, *Timočka buna, 1883 godine: uspomene* [The Timok rebellion of 1883: memoirs] (Belgrade, 1923), 62.

7. For a discussion of the party press, see Jovanović, *Vlada Milana*, III, 22ff.

8. For a discussion in the Skupština of the possible threat that the defenders of the Paris Commune represented, see *Protokoli Narodne Skupštine* (Belgrade, 1871), 84-85, 131, 509, 553.

9. Among the works of Western European authors translated were: Benjamin Constant, *The Principles of Politics and Concerning Ministerial Responsibility*; J. Bluntschli, *The Character and Spirit of Political Parties*; and Ch. Hever, *Switzerland: Her Constitution, Government and Her Self-Government.*

10. For a brief but detailed study of Serbian electoral laws, see Živojin P. Ristić, *Izborni zakoni Srbije* (Belgrade, 1935).

11. *Ibid.*, 141.

12. *Ibid.*, 100.

13. *Ibid.*, 142-45.

Chapter VII

1. See Živan Živanović, *Politička istorija Srbije*, II, 180-81. For his discussion of Progressive rule (1880-1887), see *ibid.*, 150-238. For a better and more detailed treatment, see Jovanović, *Vlada Milana*, III, 27-383.

2. See Živanović, *op. cit.*, II, 188 for some statistics.

3. Jovanović, *Vlada Milana*, III, 31.

4. Something like this was attempted in England in the eighteenth century.

5. Jovanović, *op. cit.*, 111n.

6. *Ibid.*, II, 437-53.

7. See my *Serbia, Nikola Pašić, and Yugoslavia*, 26ff. The Timok rebellion is discussed in a number of works, including those cited by Slobodan Jovanović and Živan Živanović. Also see the work of one of the members of the Radical Main Committee, Raša Milošević, *Timočka buna 1883 godine: uspomene* (Belgrade, 1923).

8. Jovanović, *Vlada Milana*, III, 163ff.

9. For a concise discussion of the war, see *ibid.*, 219-314. Also of interest is Živanović, *Politička istorija*, II, 239-89.

10. Jovanović, *op. cit.*, 341-46.

11. For a discussion of their difficulties, their divorce, and politically related events, see *ibid.*, 366-79 and 384-442.

12. For a brief account of the legislation of the Radical Skupština, see *ibid.*, 414-20.

13. On the Constitution of 1888, see Milovoje Popović, *Poreklo i postanak ustave od 1888 godine* [The origin and birth of the constitution of 1888] (Belgrade, 1937); for a Serbian text, see Jaša M. Prodanović, *Ustavne borbe*, 306-36.

14. For a text of the letter, see Grgur Jakšić, *Iz novije Srpske istorije: abdikacija Kralja Milan i druge rasprave* [From the more recent Serbian history: abdication of King Milan and other discourses] (Belgrade, 1953), 193-96.

Chapter VIII

1. For a detailed discussion of initial Radical legislation, see Slobodan Jovanović, *Vlada Aleksandra Obrenovića* [The reign of Alexander Obrenović] (3 vols., Belgrade, 1934, 1935, 1936), I, 1-170. Also see Živan Živanović, *Politička istorija*, III, 24ff. For a lucid account by a Radical, see *Prva godina novoga ustava u Srbiji* [First year of the new constitution in Serbia] (Belgrade, 1890).

2. See Jovanović, *op. cit.*, 104ff.

3. Živanović, *op. cit.*, III, 55-57.

4. *Ibid.*

5. For a discussion of Milan's financial woes, see Grgur Jakšić, *Iz novije Srpske istorije*, 206-36.

6. For a discussion, see Jovanović, *Vlada Aleksandra*, I, 298-338.

7. The best work on the coup is Raša Milošević, *Državni udar ozgo: prvi April 1893: svrnuće krnjeg kraljevskog namestništva* [State coup from above: April first 1893:dethronement of the truncated royal regency] (Belgrade, 1936). For a good brief treatment, see Jovanović, *op. cit.*, 339-420.

8. Jakšić, *op. cit.*, 227.

9. For a partial text, see *ibid.*, 228-30. This exchange of correspondence between Milan and Natalie was first published in *Le Temps* and after that in *Revue de Paris* in 1909.

10. Jakšić, *op. cit.*, 231.

11. Jovanović, *Vlada Aleksandra*, I, 353-54.

12. Pašić's unpublished manuscript, "Moja politička ispovest: beleške za brošuru," [My political confession: notes for a brochure] (written about 1902), 15.

13. See Živanović, *Politička istorija*, especially second half of volume III, and Jovanović, *op. cit.*, II, 1-244.

14. Pašić says that editing was in part at fault because he had written that he had opposed the policies of Milan's Progressive cabinet and not Milan as king or as a person. *Moja politička ispovest*, 23.

15. Živanović, *op. cit.*, IV, 87. The son resigned rather than accept such humiliation.

16. *Ibid.*, 190.

17. See Jovanović, *Vlada Aleksandra*, II, 268ff.

18. Živanović, *op. cit.*, 64.

19. For a good brief discussion, see Jovanović, *op. cit.*, 351-82.

20. For a detailed discussion of the affair, as well as theories, see *ibid.*, 406-67; 499-520.

21. For a summary of Pašić's explanation of his statement to the court and the reasoning behind it, see my *Serbia, Nikola Pašić, and Yugoslavia*, 54-57.

22. See Živanović, *Politička istorija*, IV, 193-234, and Jovanović, *Vlada Aleksandra*, III, 1-97.

23. As quoted in Živanović, *op. cit.*, 228.

24. On the constitution, see Jovanović, *op. cit.*, III, 98-138. For a Serbian text, see Jaša M. Prodanović, *Ustavne borbe*, 380-97.

25. On the elections, see Jovanović, *op. cit.*, III, 138-44.

26. The best work on the conspiracy is Dragiša Vasić, *Devetsto treća: Majski prevrat* [Nineteen three: the May overthrow] (Belgrade, 1925). A long but biased and often untrustworthy account of Vladan Djordjević's years as prime minister is his *Kraj jedne dinastije: prilozi za istoriju Srbije* [The end of a dynasty: contributions to the history of Serbia] (3 vols., Belgrade, 1905, 1906).

Chapter IX

1. See Dimitrije Djordjević, "Parlamentarna kriza u Srbiji 1905 godine," *Istoriski Časopis*, XIV-XV (1963-1965), 157-71.

2. Some of the pensioned officers were returned to the army at the time of the Balkan wars.

3. See Jovan M. Jovanović, *Borba za narodno ujedinjenje, 1903-1908* [Struggle for national union] (Belgrade, 1938), 139.

4.See his autobiography, Djordje Karadjordjević, *Istina o mome životu* [The truth about my life] (Belgrade, 1969), 184, 203, 208, 209.

5. *Ibid.*, 156, 159, 184, 194.

6. *Ibid.*, 201-203.

7. For a fuller discussion of the civil-military conflict, see my *Serbia, Nikola Pašić, and Yugoslavia* (New Brunswick, N. J., 1974), 76-85.

8. Its constitution, list of members, etc., were found among the effects of Colonel Dragutin Dimitrijević-Apis at the time of his arrest in December 1916.

9. See Vojislav J. Vučković, "Unutrašnje krize Srbije i prvi svetski rat" [Serbia's internal crises and the first world war], *Istoriski Časopis*, XIV-XV (1963-1965), 179.

10. Slobodan Jovanović, *Moji savremenici: Nikola Pašić* [My contemporaries: Nikola Pašić] (Windsor, 1962), 71.

11. Vučković, *op. cit.*, 191.

12. *Ibid.*, 186.

13. *Ibid.*, 188.

14. *Ibid.*, 188-189.

15. Slobodan Jovanović, *Nikola Pašić*, 71-74.

16. Vučković, *op. cit.*, 215.

17. See my discussion of the Salonika trial in *Serbia, Nikola Pašić, and Yugoslavia*, 81-86.

18. For a more amplified but brief survey of Serbia's foreign affairs problems following the turn of the century, see *ibid.*, 90-109.

19. The best and most thorough treatment of the tariff war is Dimitrije Djordjević, *Carinski rat Austro-Ugarske i Srbije, 1906-1911* (Belgrade, 1962).

20. For an excellent discussion of events preceding the annexation, see Wayne S. Vucinich, *Serbia Between East and West: The Events of 1903-1908* (Stanford, Calif., 1954). Also see Bernadotte E. Schmitt, *The Annexation of Bosnia, 1908-1909* (Cambridge, 1937).

21. There are many works dealing with the causes of World War I. The following are only a few, chosen somewhat at random: Oscar Jászi, *The Dissolution of the Habsburg Monarchy* (Chicago, 1929); Luigi Albertini, *The Origins of the War of 1914* (2 vols., New York, 1952, 1953); Vladimir Dedijer, *The Road to Sarajevo* (New York, 1966); Camille Bloch, *The Causes of the World War* (New York, 1968); Joachim Remak (ed.), *The First World War: Causes, Conduct, Consequences* (New York, 1971).

22. See John Clinton Adams, *Flight in Winter* (Princeton, 1942).

23. Henry Barby, *Bregalnica; Srpsko-Bulgarski Rat 1913* (Belgrade, 1914), 176.

1. Dragoslav Stranjaković, *Vučiceva buna*, 1842 (Belgrade, 1936), 7-10.

2. *Ibid.*, 11-12.

3. As quoted in *ibid.*, 22-23.

4. For a discussion of the factors in their leaving and returning, see *ibid.*, 29-40.

5. *Ibid.*, 50ff.

6. *Ibid.*, 55-57.

7. *Ibid.*, 70-71.

8. *Ibid.*, 72-73.

9. For a discussion of the reasons leading to Mihailo's fall, see *ibid.*, 84-98.

10. Slobodan Jovanović, *Ustavobranitelji i njihova vlada, 1838-1858* (Belgrade, 1912), 267-278.

11. *Ibid.*, 253-258.

12. *Ibid.*, 259-266.

13. According to one account, Blaznavac had proposed to the hastily called meeting of the temporary regency and ministers that Milan be proclaimed Prince. When all the others indicated opposition, Blaznavac alllegedly slapped his sword and angrily shouted: "Then this will decide." See Živan Živanović, *Politička istorija Srbije u drugoj polovini devetnaestog veka* (Belgrade, 1923), Vol. I, 209.

14. See Slobodan Jovanović, *Vlada Milana Obrenovića* (Belgrade, 1934), Vol. I, 1-21.

15. Blaznavac married Katarina after Mihailo's assassination.

16. Jovanović, *Vlada Milana*, Vol. I, 84-134.

17. *Ibid.*, 265-268.

18. *Ibid.*, 288.

19. *Ibid.*, Vol. II, 363-364.

20. *Ibid.*, Vol. III, 337.

21. *Ibid.*, 486-487.

22. Slobodan Jovanović, *Vlada Aleksandra Obrenovića* (Belgrade, 1934), Vol. II, 250ff, 312ff; Vol. III, 18-25.

23. Slobodan Jovanović, *Druga vlada Miloša i Mihaila, 1858-1868* (Belgrade, 1923), 277.

24. Unfortunately, much of the writing is not too helpful. The book *Pukovnik Apis* [Colonel Apis, who was executed at Salonika in 1917], (Belgrade, 1955), by Milan Ž. Živanović, for example, contains over 600 pages but nowhere does the author raise the most fundamental question: the proper role of the military in a democratic system.

25. For an informative analysis, see pamphlet by Dragoljub Jovanović, *Socialna struktura Srbije* (Belgrade, 1932).

26. See my *Serbia, Nikola Pašić, and Yugoslavia*, 79-86.

Chapter XI

1. See my "Leadership and Politics: Nineteenth Century Serbia," *The Journal of Politics*, 37 (May, 1975), 344-61.

2. Milan Grol, *Iz predratne Srbije: utisci i sećanja o vremenu i ljudima* [From Prewar Serbia: Impressions and Remembrances of the Time and Men] (Belgrade, 1939), 115-17.

3. See his "Culture and Political Development: Herder's Suggestive Insights," *American Political Science Review*, 63 (June 1969), 379-97.

4. See the excellent study on this point by Richard A. Pride, *Origins of Democracy: A Cross-National Study of Mobilization, Party Systems, and Democratic Stability* (Beverly Hills, Calif., 1970), 744.

5. See Samuel P. Huntington, "Political Development and Political Decay," *World Politics* XVII (April, 1965), 386-430.

6. "The Change to Change: Modernization, Development, and Politics," *Comparative Politics*, 3 (April, 1971), 283-322.

INDEX